The Shochu Handbook
An Introduction to Japan's Indigenous Distilled Drink

by

Christopher Pellegrini

TELEMACHUS PRESS

The Shochu Handbook: An Introduction to Japan's Indigenous Distilled Drink

Cover Designed by: Telemachus Press, LLC

Cover photos and all interior photography by Marcus Lovitt.

Proofreading by Stephen Lyman.

Published by: Telemachus Press, LLC
http://www.telemachuspress.com

Visit the author website:
http://www.shochu.pro

ISBN: 978-1-940745-27-5 (eBook)
ISBN: 978-1-940745-28-2 (paperback)

Version 2014.07.20

This book is dedicated to my parents, Lucy and Raymond.
They taught me always to give more
than I ever thought I could.

Contents

Preface

Not long after arriving in Japan in 2002, I noticed the beautiful 1.8 liter bottles on display in izakaya and restaurants around Tokyo. The calligraphy on the labels entranced me, and the size of the bottles signaled that some serious fun was within reach. Having started my career in the drinks industry as an apprentice at a small brewery in Vermont, I am burdened with an intense appreciation of both the art and science of making fine tipples, and my affinity for alcohol tasty enough to warrant packaging in a receptacle larger than a magnum basically guaranteed that I would attempt to sample and understand them all.

Some of the bars that I visited early on had lengthy nihonshu (saké) menus, and I greatly enjoyed the tutorials I was treated to by the bar staff and nearby customers about the different grades and how it's made. I purchased some English-language books about nihonshu and was able to verify much of what I had heard. My fondness of nihonshu continues to grow to this day.

Other establishments had a stronger focus on a lesser known drink that is also made in Japan, *shochu*. As the labels shared the artistry of their nihonshu counterparts, I required assistance with telling them apart at first. And I soon discovered that I wasn't able to get my head around this shape-shifting drink. I was introduced to myriad types, and shochu evaded simple description. Even more confounding was the lack of information that was available about it. There were only a few books written about shochu in Japanese, and none in English. Wikipedia was still in its infancy and hadn't expanded enough to have anything to say on the subject.

But the so-called "Third Shochu Boom" (*daisanji* shochu *būmu*) was just getting underway, and I was far from immune from the furor. Starting around 2003, shochu bars popped up all over Tokyo, some with menus boasting hundreds of labels, and one by one I found myself drinking my way through the multitude of ingredients used to make this mysterious drink. One night I'd focus on barley, and the next time out I'd find a place where I could query three or four potato shochu. Soon friends were texting me details about local watering holes with good selections of brown sugar shochu or awamori. My interest was piqued by the nuanced aromas in these different drinks, and the staggering variety of flavors left me spellbound. Shochu had me hooked.

I must add that I began my journey into the world of shochu with next to no Japanese reading or writing ability. I was making steady progress in my ability to communicate thanks to the friendly folks enjoying shochu alongside me, but it took me several years before I could discontinue my dependence on just a mental facsimile of the label's color and all those contiguous brush strokes. The bar visits were eventually supplemented by distillery tours and sit-downs with the very people who have made shochu their lives and livelihoods. They reminded me of the passionate people that I worked with at the brewery several years prior, and their love of their vocation inspired me to dig deeper.

Seeking more expert insight, I began studying for the shochu sommelier certification exam that is offered by the Sake Service Institute here in Japan, a process that brought me face to face with my old nemesis, *kanji*. It was a slow, and at times frustrating, education because it was nearly impossible for me to corroborate the things that I was learning with anything in my native tongue. Early on, the only mention that I could find of the drink was a brief and outdated summary in Richard Hosking's irreplaceable *"A Dictionary of Japanese Food."* A decade later, Andrew Dornenburg and Karen Page's amazing *"What to Drink with What You Eat"* joined my home library, and despite featuring a photo of a famous rice shochu alongside an elegant flight of sushi, the word 'shochu' fails to make an appearance. The linguistic challenges and outright lack of information that slowed me down at every turn are the reason that I decided to write this book.

I eventually prevailed on the certification exam, and I'm excited to be a member of a tiny group of licensed, non-Japanese sommeliers living in shochu's homeland. I now spend a fair amount of my time trying to spread the word about this delicious libation, its versatility, and that dizzying spectrum of flavors.

Before I go any further, though, there are a few folks that deserve some love. My family and friends have been integral in bringing this book to fruition. My wife, Yong-nam, put up with my obsessing over the minutiae of this project for the better part of three years and helped me train my palate for the tasting exam somewhere in between. My family in Vermont, Lucy Pellegrini, Scott Pellegrini, and Kate and Aaron Welch, were my backbone from afar.

To Thatcher and Junko Spero, David Groff, Garrett DeOrio, Kozo Ota, David Watkins, and Mac Salman—the jovial encouragement was greatly appreciated. And to Marcus Lovitt and Mieko Higano, the heart and soul of the Japan Eats team, thank you for helping me reach the finish line. You know as well as anyone how crazy this trip has been. The talented folks at Telemachus Press, who have been doggedly diligent and patient throughout this process, also receive perpetual hat-tips for pretending like I was always on schedule. Stephen Lyman, my shochu doppelganger from afar, helped tidy up the manuscript with his detailed notes—your insight was much appreciated. I'd also like to thank the regular members of my CAST Meetup group in Tokyo for their continued support of the drive to bring shochu to a wider audience.

As far as corporate friends in Japan go, I would like to extend hugs to the Yasuda Photo Studio team (http://yasudaphotostudio.com/) who graciously provided studio space and equipment to help make the bottle photos pop. I owe you some kilned shochu cups. And if they didn't already own tons of them, I'd offer the same to the staff at Kuroki Honten, Satsuma Shuzō, and Satsuma Musō. Your passion and attention to detail have inspired me immeasurably. I will visit again soon, I promise.

And to you, dear reader! Thank you for reading this far. Over the next several chapters I hope to demystify shochu for you and answer most of the questions I can imagine are now on the tip of your tongue. I'd be willing to bet that they were exactly the same things running through my mind when I was first drawn in by this unique drink.

Introduction

Welcome to the World of Shochu and Awamori!
This book was written with many people in mind. While its utility will be more readily apparent to readers living or traveling in Japan, far-flung Japan enthusiasts and shochu drinkers alike will find plenty here to make them want to book a table at the nearest Japanese restaurant or even a flight to shochu's homeland.

This is certainly a book that can be read out of order—although I must warn you that I have taken significant strides to eliminate redundancy in the number of times that key vocabulary and production concepts are explained. At some point most readers will find it necessary to go back and read chapters that they skipped. However, dog-earing the Glossary at the back of the book should help bridge some of the gaps.

For people living/traveling in Japan, the following chapters may be of particular interest:
Chapter 5: **Reading the label** is for when you find yourself in front of a wall of shochu at your local market.
Chapter 6: **How to serve shochu** is for when you get your purchases back to your abode.

Chapter 8: **Recommended shochu** is for when you decide that you don't yet have enough shochu and need to go back.

Chapter 9: **Shochu recipes** is for times when you feel like being more creative.

Chapter 10: **Basic Japanese for shochu drinkers** is absolutely essential for speaking the language of shochu.

For anyone in the world who wants to understand the subtleties of the different varieties of the drink:

Chapter 4: **Types of shochu** will explain the different distillation types and most popular ingredients.

Chapter 7: **Shochu pairing and sharing** will supply the reader with shochu tasting vocabulary and meal tips.

The beginning of chapter 10 is probably worth a quick look for anyone who is unsure of how to read transliterated Japanese words. The primer on Japanese vowel sounds and pronunciation should boost your confidence when facing the essential vocabulary of the shochu world.

There's also a lot in store here for anyone working in the restaurant and bar industry. If you've ever felt like you need help talking about the Japanese drinks that you're serving, then this book should definitely help. You'll find assistance with explaining: the differences between shochu and other drinks in the first two chapters; the basics of the production process in chapter three; and pairing and describing flavors in chapter seven.

Chapter 1: **What is shochu?** Included are a history of shochu's evolution and a rundown of how it differs from nihonshu (saké).

Chapter 2: **How is honkaku shochu unique?** This chapter will help you explain how shochu is unlike the other clear spirits of the world.

Chapter 3: **How is shochu made?** This will help you get your head around how those complex aromas and flavors are created.

Chapter 7: **Shochu pairing and sharing** is a good starting point for those who need help with describing flavors.

A couple of linguistic disclaimers:

There are no English-style plurals in the Japanese language, so I have consciously avoided using words like 'shochus' in this book. In other words, "We had shochu with dinner" and "The shop now boasts more than 30 shochu" are both correct.

Those readers with some knowledge of the Japanese language will quickly notice that I have carefully included macrons over elongated vowels in all situations except for two sets of Japanese vocabulary. One is proper nouns. Even though it would be more consistent to include them over words like *Tokyo*, I have elided them because macrons are exceedingly rare over such words in the real world. The second group is comprised of words that I believe will be adopted into other languages and eventually leave their macrons behind anyway. The shining star of this group is undoubtedly *shochu* which, for posterity's sake, makes an appearance in the glossary at the end of this book with its macrons intact.

Thank you!

Maybe you're here because of an interest in drinks in general and Japanese culture in particular. Alternatively, maybe you already know a thing or two about how alcohol is made, or you are lucky enough to work in an establishment that is now selling shochu. Perhaps you're even one of those readers who has tried shochu a couple of times but has been unsatisfied with the vague and conflicting drink descriptions offered by the menu and wait staff that you dealt with the night prior. Read on, for I'm pretty sure that most of your questions will be answered in the next few chapters of this book. Thanks for joining me, and welcome to the world of Japan's ubiquitous libation, shochu!

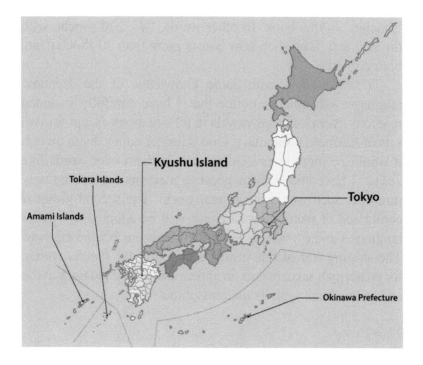

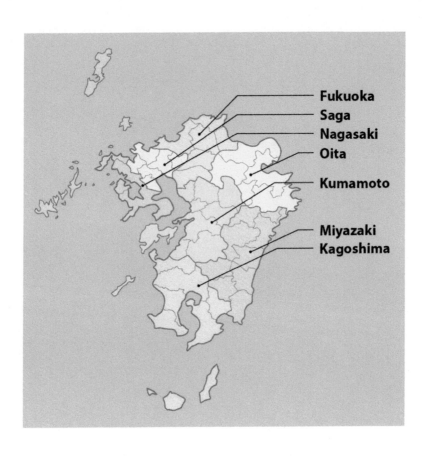

Chapter 1
What is shochu?

Shochu is good. Often referred to by its statelier moniker, "honkaku shochu," it's Japan's oldest distilled alcoholic beverage. It's made from a variety of ingredients, everything from sweet potatoes to brown sugar to chestnuts (and their *kōji*), and it's a mainstay in most bars, restaurants, and bottle shops around the country. An alleged relative of the continental distilling traditions commonly referred to as *arak*, shochu's most direct ancestor is the awamori that is produced and adored in the *Ryūkyū* Islands, a part of Japan that is now known as Okinawa. It is a beverage that is intimately connected to the subtleties of Japanese cuisine and the vegetation that calls this country home.

Aside from being delicious, what else is shochu? Well, it's easy to pronounce correctly. Say it with me, *show-chew* (or try /shōh chū/ if you have already perused the first part of chapter 10). The Chinese characters (*kanji*) used to write the word on bottles and menus here in Japan, 焼酎, literally mean 'burned alcohol' which alludes to the fact that it's distilled. This may come as a surprise for some readers, but despite the strong sales and recognition afforded to Japanese whiskey around the world these days, shochu is currently the best-selling spirit here in Japan. After decades of playing second fiddle to nihonshu (saké), this versatile beverage seems to finally be enjoying the respect that it deserves.

Indeed, versatility is a major reason why shochu is climbing the ranks. It's an excellent aperitif but is also commonly enjoyed alongside a meal. It goes without saying that shochu is great when drinking socially, and it can be served in myriad ways. People drink it straight up, as the base alcohol in a cocktail, with a couple splashes of cool water, and even with hot water to help enhance the drink's bouquet. The ability to suit any occasion or craving is what causes it to show up in nearly every convenience store, supermarket, restaurant, bar and bottle shop across Japan, and it's also why it will soon be seen on the menu of a drinking establishment near you.

And what is shochu *not*? Well, at 50-60 proof, it certainly doesn't qualify for membership in the world's "firewater" club, that legion of spirits whose credentials include blinding alcohol percentages and searing aftertaste—and membership *dues* involve multi-day hangovers. On the contrary, shochu is a respected tipple that has been granted geographical protection by the World Trade Organization (WTO) to help prevent others from passing their beverages off as the real thing. Just as wine can only be labeled Bordeaux if it was brewed in that particular region of France, and Scotch whiskey must be distilled in Scotland, there are four types of shochu and awamori that enjoy the same international protection under Article 23 of the TRIPS agreement.

History
Historians have found evidence of distillation technology being used in Mesopotamia, which is now modern-day Iraq, between four and five thousand years ago. However, it took quite a while for that technology to spread around the world. Distillation was taking place in Cordoba, Spain by 732 BC, and eastern trade routes helped give rise to distillation in India roughly 400 years later. Japan was first introduced to the wonderful world of distilled spirits in the early 15th century, and official records kept by Korea's Joseon Dynasty show that by 1477 Okinawans were making their own distilled drinks to compete with the variety of alcoholic beverages being imported through decades of trade with Siam (modern-day Thailand).

No one is entirely sure how distillation technology finally made its way to Japan, but there are at least four major theories that are still being debated. The most popular theory is the overseas route between Thailand and Okinawa, Japan. This route seems the most probable because of Okinawa's trade history, as well as the initial and continued use of long-grain Thai rice in the production of shochu's sibling spirit to the south, awamori.

The rest of the possible routes find their way to Japan via China. The first hypothesizes an arcing journey that passes through northern China before traveling down through the Korean Peninsula and eventually taking a short trip across the water to Kyushu Island, an area that would eventually become the heart and soul of shochu production in Japan. It is highly likely that this route had a direct hand in the birth of Japan's barley shochu tradition. A more southerly route swings past modern-day Shanghai, skips the peninsula, and sails straight to Kyushu. The final theory posits that distillation techniques journeyed across southern China before eventually landing at the ports of Okinawa's main island. Even though historians may never settle on a definitive connection to the distilling bloodline of the Asian continent, it's probably fair to assume that all four of these routes, with all of the goods and ideas that changed hands along them, had at least a small influence on the birth of distilled drinks in Japan at one point or another.

Following the official Korean accounts of trade and life in Okinawa during the fifteenth century, Jorge Álvarez, a Portuguese explorer who spent time in Yamagawa Port near the mouth of Kagoshima Bay, wrote in 1546 that the Japanese drank an *arak*-like spirit made from rice. This is likely the first reference to rice shochu, and Álvarez further commented that he never witnessed a single display of public drunkenness. The reason for this, he wrote, was that when the local residents became inebriated, they simply made themselves comfy and conked out.

In 1954, the earliest known direct reference to shochu was discovered at a shrine in northern Kagoshima Prefecture. The carpenters of the Koriyama Hachiman Shrine vented their frustrations with the head priest by inscribing some graffiti on one of the structure's internal boards. The graffiti, dating from 1559, is written in an old style of Japanese that is no longer used, but my translation of the modern Japanese equivalent would be, "The chief shintō priest of the shrine was so stingy that he never once gave us shochu to drink."

By 1696 some brewers were already adding shochu to their nihonshu, a practice that continues in some grades to this day. However, it wasn't until 1705 that the sweet potato, which was called *kansho* (甘藷) back then, finally reached its enduring home in Japan, southern Kyushu Island, on Riemon Maeda's return trip from the islands of Okinawa. The spud spread quickly. In 1723 it had made its way all the way out to Hachijojima near the end of the Izu Islands south of Tokyo. In 1734, sweet potatoes were brought to Tokyo itself (back then call Edo), and the Tosa region (modern-day Kochi Prefecture on Shikoku Island) was the recipient of both sweet potatoes and shochu distillation know-how in 1735. Hachijojima, on the other hand, had to wait until 1853 for still technology to reach its volcanic shores.

A serving carafe called a *gara* from Kumamoto Prefecture.

In 1895 the patent still (continuous distillation) arrived in Japan, and in 1910 multiple-distilled shochu (*kōrui*) hit the market, setting the groundwork for countless innovations and improvements in the traditional single-distilled (*otsurui*) shochu industry. Some of the more momentous occasions were the discovery of white *kōji kin* by Gen'ichiro Kawachi in 1923, and the official recognition of brown sugar shochu in 1953. However, it took until the 1970s for single-distilled shochu to start commanding the respect it deserved. Shochu makers started using the current designation *honkaku* in 1971, and they also began experimenting with different ingredients and low pressure (*gen'atsu*) distillation. Best-selling shochu labels such as Unkai (*soba* shochu) and Iichiko (barley shochu) were born in 1973 and 1979, respectively, and popular sesame and *gen'atsu* shochu reached the market in the interim.

Many scholars point to 1976 as the beginning of the first shochu boom in Japan. This was roughly the same time that the now standard hot water (*oyuwari*) mixing ratio of 6:4 (*roku yon*) was popularized, and later a pair of legendary aged barley shochu from Kuroki Honten and Satsuma Shuzō helped reinvigorate the shochu boom in the 1980s. November 1st, 1987, was the first year that Honkaku Shochu and Awamori Day was celebrated. That inaugural celebration was held right about when the GATT and TRIPS negotiations began their ongoing search for international common ground on recognizing and protecting intellectual property rights. This had significant ramifications for the shochu and awamori industries because rules for using regional names to add value to products were codified in the final agreement, and as mentioned earlier Japan now boasts four appellations of origin ascribed to shochu and awamori products.

Cask-aged shochu stacked to the ceiling.

The third and most recent so-called 'Shochu Boom' swept the major metropolitan regions of Japan starting in 2003. Honkaku shochu bars and izakaya blossomed around Tokyo, some of which offered customers shochu lists of literally hundreds of bottles. The selection at most supermarkets, and even at many convenience stores, has followed suit with label inventories reaching up into the dozens in some establishments.

Shochu is now produced in all 47 of Japan's prefectures, but the primary centers of production are still the prefectures of Kyushu Island (honkaku shochu) and Okinawa Prefecture (awamori). Kyushu is made up of seven prefectures, each with its own forte in terms of the ingredients locally available to the distiller. Oita, Fukuoka, and Saga Prefectures in the north are known for their *kasutori* shochu which is distilled from nihonshu lees. Kumamoto Prefecture is also acclaimed for its rice shochu products although lees are not used. Oita Prefecture again, and Nagasaki and Miyazaki Prefectures as well, make very tasty barley shochu. Miyazaki also gets credit for introducing the world to buckwheat shochu while concurrently producing a fair amount of sweet potato shochu. However, the latter type of shochu is completely dominated by neighboring Kagoshima Prefecture, Kyushu's most southern member. The Amami Islands that extend toward Okinawa Prefecture are technically part of Kagoshima, so the prefecture can claim brown sugar shochu as well. Okinawa Prefecture used to make potato shochu hundreds of years ago, but these days it focuses almost exclusively on distilling and aging awamori.

All of these references to shochu and awamori, when added together, show that the history of these drinks exceeds five hundred years. Many are surprised when they hear that shochu has been around for so long and played such an important role in society given that the drink has only recently begun to find its way outside of Japan. Over the past several decades, shochu consumption in Japan has surged to the extent that supply is just barely keeping up with demand. This is not particularly good news for shochu fans outside of Japan. It is likely that they will never be able to get their hands on some of the finer specimens cooked up by tiny family-run distilleries in the southwestern prefectures of the archipelago. However, if history is any indication, and it often is with aspects of Japanese culinary and entertainment culture, shochu is gearing up for a steady expansion to all corners of the globe, including a bottle shop or restaurant near you.

How is shochu different from *saké*?

But before we go any further, let's get one thing straight—shochu should never be confused with nihonshu. This is something that countless people from the shochu and nihonshu industries in Japan have asked me to stress when they learned that I was writing this book. Nihonshu, which is known as saké outside of Japan and sometimes called *seishu* domestically, is a drink brewed from polished rice. Quite simply, shochu is distilled, but nihonshu is not. Puzzlingly, nihonshu is often referred to as a rice wine due to the lack of carbonation in most varieties, but it is not technically a wine in any way, shape, or form. Actually, if you're in the food and drinks industry and your business serves nihonshu, then you should definitely stop calling it rice wine. Let consumers make that mistake so that you can politely correct them and explain that the nihonshu brewing process is far more complicated than what is required for wine production. And please learn to pronounce saké correctly (*sah-keh*).

In fact, since we're splitting hairs here, nihonshu is probably more similar to beer than wine at least as far as the brewing process itself is concerned. But don't go calling it a rice beer either. That would effectively equate nihonshu with the rice lagers of the world, and that's just not a polite thing to do. To avoid getting bogged down in the minute differences between beer, nihonshu, and wine production, and to avoid self-righteous, alcohol-fueled warfare, let us simply cut this short by accepting nihonshu expert and author John Gauntner's assertion that his beverage of choice is neither a beer nor a wine—it deserves a classification all its own.

Honkaku shochu, on the other hand, is far easier to classify. It's a spirit, and most types of shochu neither smell nor taste anything like nihonshu. To be fair, shochu has a few modest ties to its more well-known cousin. For instance, rice is one of the four most common base ingredients used to make shochu, and nihonshu lees are used to make one particular variety of shochu called *kasutori*. Awamori, the shochu made in Okinawa, is also made with rice. Additionally, the same variety of *kōji kin* that is used to break rice starch down into fermentable sugars is currently used in several popular shochu. Now that may sound like a lot of similarities, but the truth of the matter is that the nose and taste buds will find very little in common between most shochu and nihonshu.

Look at it this way: rice shochu is to nihonshu what whiskey is to beer and brandy is to wine. But that obscenely simplified comparison falls apart when you look at all of the different ingredients used to make honkaku shochu. I defy thee to sip a potato shochu, or a kelp shochu, or a shiitake mushroom shochu and remark with a straight face that they remind you either of nihonshu or each other. There is simply no intellectually or alcoholically honest way to think of shochu and nihonshu as being the same thing, or in the vast majority of cases, even remotely similar. So don't.

Accordingly, it is correct to group shochu with all of the other spirits of the world. That's right, shochu will one day find its way into your local liquor shop on a shelf right beside the whiskey, rum, gin, vodka, and tequila. And by the way, *saké* is actually the Japanese word for 'alcohol,' so shochu, wine, whiskey, and beer are saké, too. To wit, if you walk into an izakaya in Kagoshima Prefecture and ask for saké, they'll serve you shochu.

What is shochu made from?
This is the mind-blowing part, and it simultaneously serves as a window to how deep the shochu rabbit hole goes. Along with its versatility, shochu lovers are infatuated with its variety. Because honkaku shochu is made from such a dizzying range of base ingredients, the resulting beverages can vary enormously. Indeed, this nearly endless variety of aroma and flavor is what makes the world of shochu so exciting and enjoyable for the enthusiast. Shochu is very much like beer in that respect.

Base ingredients used in honkaku shochu production:

sweet potato (*satsuma imo*)	barley (*mugi*)	rice (*kome*)	brown sugar (*kokutō*
buckwheat (*soba*)	aloe (*aroe*)	pumpkin (*kabocha*)	milk (*gyūnyū*)
chestnut (*kuri*)	sesame (*goma*)	carrot (*ninjin*)	kelp (*konbu*)
perilla (*shiso*)	cactus (*saboten*)	tomato	radish (*daikon*)

That short list was about one-fifth of the legally recognized raw ingredients used to make honkaku shochu here in Japan. Obviously, some types are more popular and common than others. Sweet potato, barley, rice (including awamori and *kasutori* shochu), buckwheat, and brown sugar are by far the biggest sellers. Other types of shochu are regional phenomena that are often marketed as souvenirs to tourists looking for local goodies. Interestingly, dates are the only fruit legally allowed in the production of honkaku shochu. My advice is to try whatever you can get your hands on. A tomato or green pepper shochu might not be your cup of tea, so to speak, but I bet you could have some fun making a signature Bloody Mary with them. Naturally, since we're dealing with such a wide swath of aroma and flavor, the food pairing possibilities are literally endless.

Sweet potatoes getting a greenhouse-assisted head start.

Japan's next cultural export
And this book? Well, the most exciting part of it for me is helping to get people outside of Japan in on the ground floor of shochu's imminent spread across the globe. Now granted, getting your hands on good shochu is still a difficult thing to do in many places, but Japanese restaurants and *izakaya* are springing up in major cities everywhere, and curious imbibers are asking their local distributors to start sourcing it. You should, too.

Shochu is still relatively new to the world of international export, and that is part of the reason why it has not yet gotten the press that it deserves. To be fair, even in Japan shochu is largely denied the media attention afforded to happenings in the beer and nihonshu industries. Interestingly, over the past decade, shochu has quietly overtaken nihonshu in terms of domestic consumption. According to the Japanese Tax Office, sales of shochu eclipsed those of nihonshu in 2003, and the gap has increased ever since. In 2009, distilleries shipped more than one million kiloliters of shochu while nihonshu brewers sold 634,000. However, despite strong evidence of shochu's position in the drinks industry, many still see it as the final stop on the long train line of old man drinks (the penultimate is single malt whiskey in case you were wondering). Things are certainly changing, albeit slowly.

One could argue that there are similarities between shochu's role in Japan's culinary culture and the position of beer in the world's collective conscious. My experience working in the beer industry taught me that no matter how refined the product we were brewing, and no matter how well it complemented the items on the restaurant menu where it was being served, people would automatically turn their attention to the wine list. There is an ingrained notion that wine is simply more sophisticated, or as beer expert, author, and educator Randy Mosher surmised, "the automatic sense of class and status accorded to wine relative to beer." To my mind, shochu is basically in the same boat as beer but looking up at nihonshu.

Allow me to leave you with some of shochu's sales points:

Compared with the spirits of the world
1. Larger variety of base ingredients used in production
2. Wider variety of flavors and aromas

3. Greater flexibility of serving styles: straight, on the rocks, mixed with cold/hot water, cocktail, etc.
4. Lower calorie content/ABV
5. Less likely to cause hangover (moderate consumption!)
6. Pairs well with all types of cuisine
7. Appropriate before, during, and after meals

Compared with other drinks produced in Japan
1. Better cost performance
2. Longer shelf life than brewed drinks
3. More flexibility in serving style to suit individual taste
4. Comparable levels of historical significance and character
5. Far greater variety of flavors and aromas
6. More flexibility when pairing with food

Chapter 2
How is honkaku shochu unique?

Due to the immense variety of ingredients and resulting aroma, flavor profile, mouth feel and finish, the casual drinker will often find it difficult to pin shochu down or categorize it. This drink is not easily pigeon-holed, that's for sure. One can sample a different bottle each day for months on end and still have only a fleeting sense of what shochu is all about. Many times the confusion can be attributed to a lack of appreciation of the varied base ingredients, production techniques, and storage methods that cause the bottled result to dance all over the palate's map.

It is a drink that, just like wine, beer and whiskey, is difficult to quantify in a summary of 140 Twitter bytes or less. Seated at your local bar, the shochu on the left might seem enormously similar to rye but the one perched right next to it is reminiscent of that milky *makgeolli* you tried at a Korean barbeque restaurant. Shochu is at once mind-boggling and joyous like that. During a recent stay in Avignon, France, I had the good fortune to dine at a small restaurant with a modest but excellent list of Côtes du Rhône wines. Imagine my delight when I found that the bouquet of my glass of "Bressy-Masson Mode Vergaderen Get Together Rencontres" was a dead ringer for a potato shochu! Wine enthusiasts, of course, will argue that it is the shochu that smells like the wine, but my point about the various liquids carrying the shochu banner stands undented. Sometimes shochu presents you with the sensory experience that you expect. Other times, a potato shochu can smell exactly like a fine wine. And that's one of its' indelible beauties—it's fully capable of blanketing the far reaches of the flavor map. Another admirable trait is its tendency not to cause severe hangovers.

The shochu industry's ability to give consumers so many different looks is precisely why it's necessary to explain how honkaku shochu is unique within the vast and well-documented world of spirits, or what is colloquially known as 'hard alcohol' or liquor in other parts of the world. Shochu is distilled and sold almost everywhere in Japan, but somehow it largely stays out of the way. That is part of the reason why only about a dozen books have been written on the subject in Japanese, of which about five of them are readily available at decent bookstores, and until this book's publication, zero had been penned in English.

What follows is a brief and necessarily simple rundown of how shochu differs from some of the other colorless spirits from across the globe.

Honkaku Shochu vs Vodka

Honkaku shochu is often erroneously referred to as 'Japanese vodka' due to the fact that it is a distilled clear beverage. One key difference is that honkaku shochu uses *kōji* to help with saccharification while mass market vodka does not. Also, and this is incredibly important, honkaku shochu is distilled just once in a pot still, but as you've probably noticed from the label vodka is generally distilled at least a few times. As we will see, distilling repeatedly will strip out most hints of whatever plant was fermented to make alcohol. Indeed, vodka is valued in cocktail mixing due to its lack of strong flavors and aromas, and that all comes down to the fact that it is distilled repeatedly.

More obvious than differences in production processes, to the casual observer at least, is the fact that honkaku shochu is commonly bottled for the Japanese market at 25% alcohol by volume (ABV) while most vodka is at least 80 proof (40% ABV). Despite its elevated ethanol content, vodka is frequently consumed straight—in wee glasses that are designed to hasten the end of the evening. To be sure, shochu is also enjoyed neat, but often in larger glasses and at a slower pace. There's simply much more to savor with each sip.

It is also worth noting that while good vodka and shochu are smooth, there is generally no comparison in terms of bouquet and flavor. You will find honkaku shochu that is incredibly smooth going down, especially low pressure distilled rice (*kome*) and some types of barley (*mugi*) shochu, but on the whole the flavors and aromas from the ingredients used to make the mash will be readily apparent. Cheaper varieties of shochu known as *kōrui* (multiple-distilled) are nondescript in their bouquet, attack, and mouthfeel and can thus be equated more closely with vodka even though they're not filtered with white birch charcoal. However, *kōrui* shochu is almost never consumed straight up or on the rocks—it's commonly used as cocktail fuel—so some might opine that it is unfair to equate it with upper tier vodka.

Honkaku Shochu vs Soju (Korea)

Traditionally made soju (*soh ju*) is more similar to honkaku shochu than vodka. As in shochu production, old-school soju distillers leverage *kōji kin* (mold spores) to provide the enzymes necessary for converting starches into sugar and the fermented mash is run through a pot still. However, the overwhelming majority of soju made today is not made in the traditional style, thus it bears little resemblance to honkaku shochu. That last claim may sound strange to some folks reading this outside of Japan. Allow me to explain.

Due to a state-specific American liquor control tax loophole, many eating and drinking establishments in the US that carry shochu, particularly in the states of California and New York, serve it under the name soju, its Korean multiple-distilled cousin. In many cases it actually says 'soju' right on the bottle. Obviously, this has had the effect of confusing and misinforming consumers. The reason for this is soju, due to its mid-level ABV and some heavy lobbying at the California state capitol, now skirts the parameters of a full-blown liquor license which can be prohibitively expensive for new business owners. Many establishments opt for the less restrictive beer and wine license which currently accommodates some medium ABV drinks like soju (24% ABV and lower).

Hence, shochu has benefitted from hiding under the soju umbrella in a handful of key markets. Reaching a wider audience by comfortably flying beneath the radar, and falsely printing 'soju' on the label, is apparently still preferable to locking horns with the rigmarole of American tax law at this juncture in shochu's nascent foray outside of Japan. However, despite being different pronunciations of the same Chinese characters, there are enormous differences between honkaku shochu and soju.

Soju, the national drink of both North and South Korea, is a multiple-distilled spirit made by massive corporations. And it is generally *not* distilled purely from rice, much to the surprise of some who count it as a regular part of their diet. Rice is expensive, and for a long time was restricted due to shortages, so to keep costs down macro-distillers such as Jinro (pronounced *'jilloh'* in Korean, believe it or not) often blend in or substitute cheaper starch substitutes such as yams and tapioca. This means that a typical 350 ml bottle of soju costs only a little over US$1.00 at most South Korean convenience and grocery stores. For those that have never tried it straight up, as people in Korea do in shot glasses (when in Korea, don't ever put ice in it!), two or three standard-size bottles are enough for most folks to forget what happened during the preceding 18 hours. According to standard Korean drinking protocol, if you can drink this much on your own plus make it home without losing any valuables, then you are deemed to have a respectable alcohol tolerance.

The small green bottles of soju that accompany many meals in Korea are chilled before serving. The reduced temperature is important—you wouldn't want to drink it warm any more than you'd welcome a pint of room-temperature Heineken. Shot glasses are employed in a very communal atmosphere to deftly move on to the next bottle at an alarming pace. Outside of Korea, on the other hand, soju, like its *kōrui* shochu counterpart, is often used as a cheap vodka substitute because it plays well with a variety of mixers.

But the color of the bottle and the size of the glass aren't really what make soju so different from honkaku shochu. At the risk of insulting soju adorers around the world, soju is totally different from honkaku shochu because the vast majority of it is designed to be cheap for both the producer and consumer. To wit, macro distillers have been dropping soju's ABV for years, one percentage point at a time, to maintain profit margins. Additionally, they often eschew the time-consuming *kōji* preparation process while blending a number of sweet and sour additives into the product to help regulate the taste and make it easier to drink.

In contrast, the traditional soju market, known in Korea as Andong Soju, is still heart-breakingly small. This is the exact opposite of the situation in Japan where honkaku shochu's robust flavors are gaining popularity and outsell the cheap stuff, additives are not used, and distillers attempt to differentiate themselves by using the best available ingredients.

As mentioned in our vodka comparison, *kōrui* shochu is distilled to the point that it loses almost all of the flavors that are preserved in its single-distilled and more expensive sibling, honkaku shochu. Consequently, *kōrui* shochu, like soju, is neutral enough to be a logical choice for cocktails both in Japan and abroad. Because they are both designed to be cheap and lacking in overall character, it is not unfair to surmise that there are serious similarities between the two.

Honkaku shochu, on the other hand, provides excellent cost-performance, and can generally compete with whiskey prices in its home market. It is not made from tapioca or molasses and never is it multiple-distilled. In other words, the drink that this book is primarily concerned with is as different from standard soju as single malt scotch is from bathtub corn moonshine. At the risk of relegating soju to a well-level spirit, honkaku shochu would more likely be found a shelf or two above the bartender's navel.

Honkaku Shochu vs Awamori

These two drinks are far more similar than any of the clear spirits mentioned earlier, and generally speaking awamori is one type of shochu. The biggest differences between them, and part of the reason why they have different names, are the specifics of the pre-distillation production process and the type of rice involved in *kōji* preparation and fermentation.

One of the rules of awamori production is that all of the ingredients are mixed into the mash at the same time. In other words, there's only one stage of fermentation (*zenkōji shikomi*). At the risk of getting ahead of ourselves here, the *kōji kin* and yeast immediately begin to tag team the starch and produce alcohol and carbon dioxide, a ridiculously complex process called multiple parallel fermentation (*heikō fukuhakkō*). However, there is no single-stage fermentation rule when it comes to the production of honkaku shochu, and these days a two-step mash process is routine. Simplifying things greatly, the first stage is smaller in volume and gives the *kōji kin* and yeast a chance to get revved up. The second stage introduces a large amount of extra fuel (starch!) to the bubbling feast, and the starch chains are immediately disassembled into fermentable sugars by the *kōji kin* and converted into alcohol by the yeast that multiplied exponentially during the first stage of fermentation. In case you were wondering, *heikō fukuhakkō* does not occur when making wine, beer, or whiskey.

As for starch supply, rice shochu uses short grained *japonica* rice while awamori is made with long grained *indica*, a clear legacy, many claim, of the drink's ancestral link to Thailand. As posited in the previous chapter, awamori was first distilled in the islands of Okinawa around Columbus's time and then spread north to Kyushu within the next century. For those not up on their elementary school history, awamori

developed in Okinawa during the 1400s and reached mainland
Japan sometime in the 1500s. That would mean that shochu is
a direct descendent of awamori.

   Also of significance is the fact that awamori tends to pack
a more robust alcoholic punch than shochu. It is standard for
awamori to hit store shelves at a bottled ABV of 30-40% which
elevates it to the mind eraser level of spirits indigenous to the
west. This is nearly always an adult-sized helping of ethanol
more than what is normal for honkaku shochu. As such,
awamori is generally served on the rocks and with a couples
splashes of water. Drinking it neat is advised only for those
who have recently lost a significant court case.
   One other peculiarity of shochu's brethren to the south is
that of aging. Aged awamori, as encoded in the prefecture's
tax scriptures, is allowed to use the designation *kūsu* (古酒:
pronounced *koshu* in most northern parts of the archipelago)
which means that at least 50% of the bottle's contents were
aged for three years or longer. This also indicates that the

bottle will be priced several echelons above the run-of-the-mill stuff which is aged six months or less, so shop accordingly. Jump forward to chapter five if you'd like more detail about *kūsu* awamori.

Another important difference between awamori and shochu involves the type of *kōji kin* that is used. The mold in question here is from the Aspergillus family, and it's the same *kōji kin* that is used in the production of nihonshu and a large number of dishes produced not only in Japan but in South Korea and China as well. Awamori, as a rule, uses only so-called black mold (*Aspergillus awamori*, or recently *Aspergillus luchuensis*) while nihonshu is made with a different color, yellow (*Aspergillus oryzae*). White mold (*Aspergillus kawachii*) is the third and most common variant used in shochu production.

A quick clarification, shochu was originally made with yellow *kōji kin*, but it's actually produced with all three types of mold these days because the ability to control the climate and conditions of the distillery has improved greatly. And yes, you did just read the word *mold* several times in the context of alcohol production. Aspergillus molds are just another way of breaking starches down into fermentable sugars for yeast to eat, a process commonly called saccharification. For those who are not familiar with the chemistry involved in alcohol production, let's just say that yeast can't handle the complex starch chains in many of the plants used to produce shochu. A couple of extra steps are required in order to turn starch to sugar so that the yeast can start the fermentation process.

Just as with beer and whiskey production, the yeast needs a little extra help. It's not as straightforward as in the production of wine where the sugars are already there for yeast to do their thing (brewer's yeast clings naturally to the outside of the grape, by the way). In the case of beer and whiskey, the grains are malted, milled, and then mixed with hot water to convert the starches into glucose, a simple sugar that yeast can turn into alcohol and carbon dioxide. With shochu, awamori, and nihonshu, on the other hand, Aspergillus mold strains take the place of malting, and this makes it possible for the yeast to do their very important job before distillation. This is, yet again, a gross over-simplification of the mind-bogglingly complicated process of multiple parallel fermentation.

Honkaku Shochu vs Rum

Brown sugar (*kokutō*) shochu, a variety that is produced in the Amami Islands off the southern coast of Kagoshima Prefecture, is very likely to remind people of rum. This makes perfect sense because sugar cane is used in the production of both spirits. The one big difference, however, is the fact that brown sugar shochu is made with a rice *kōji* starter mash, and rum is not. Actually, most *kokutō* shochu is not as sweet as one might expect due to the influence of the *kōji*. Furthermore, the most ubiquitous rum labels on the international market, such as Bacardi, Captain Morgan, or Havana Club, are bottled at a higher alcohol content, anywhere from 70 to 100 proof. Brown sugar shochu, on the other hand, generally finds its way into your liquor cabinet at 50-60 proof (25-30% ABV).

Conclusion

Shochu, more than its distilled relatives from around the world, is a dizzyingly diverse tipple. If you read the back label and figure out what the base ingredient and *kōji* variety are, then you might be able to concoct an educated guess about what you are about to enjoy. But just like a craft beer or fine wine, you will not truly know what you're in for until that second or third sip. As will be revealed in the following chapters, shochu has a far wider range of aromas and flavors than any of the clear spirits mentioned thus far. If you're the type of person who enjoys complexity, variety, and layers in their drinks, then shochu is right up your alley.

Chapter 3
How is honkaku shochu made?

Distilled beverages aren't nearly as old as beer or wine, but their development is no less integral to the history of humankind. Originally used as medicinal remedies in the middle ages, and also for making perfumes and balms, it was not long before their full value became known to not only the scientists of Central Asia, but also the citizens. Many cultures worked with and developed the still technology that helped usher the advancement of both early pharmacology and general conduct disorderly.

The distillation techniques brought to southern Kyushu in the 16th century were adapted to fit the climate and natural resources of the region. At first, the most common starches used in shochu production were actually rice (*kome*) and barley (*mugi*). Barley has enjoyed enduring popularity over the centuries with its most recent boom taking place in the 1970s. More recently, however, a family of spuds has thrown its collective hat into the ring to vie for the shochu-loving public's attention. This starch-packed vegetable from South America, the sweet potato (*satsuma imo*), arrived and was found to be perfectly suited to the Kyushu climate and terrain. The rest, as they say, is history, and Satsuma Shochu has since received appellation of origin protection from the WTO. Many other base ingredients are used, but these days distilleries sell four times as much sweet potato and barley shochu as rice shochu.

Shochu production techniques vary widely based both on the ingredients involved and the prerogatives of the head brewer (*tōji*), so let's start with an in-depth but easy to understand exploration of how sweet potato shochu is typically produced. The production of honkaku shochu, no matter what the principal ingredient may be, generally follows this pattern:

1. *Kōji* preparation
2. First *moromi* fermentation
3. Second *moromi* fermentation
4. Distillation
5. Aging
6. Before bottling
   a. *Dilution*
   b. *Filtration*
7. Bottling

1. *Kōji* preparation (*seigiku*)

As mentioned in chapter two, Aspergillus mold, referred to here as *kōji kin*, is an essential part of the magic that allows fermentation to take place. In the creation of alcohol, whether it's wine, beer or shochu, sugar reacts with yeast to create alcohol. For wine, grapes provide the sugar, and as mentioned in the last chapter the yeast is able to get started right away turning it into alcohol. However, beer requires an extra step before fermentation can take place. This is simplifying things immeasurably, but basically the grains are soaked and allowed to germinate, and then the sprouting process is quickly halted through the use of high temperatures so that the starches inside the grains can be easily modified into sugars with the help of some hot water (sorry, that's *liquor* to you old-school brewer types). Grains that have undergone this process are known as 'malt.'

There are, of course, other ways of converting starches into fermentable sugars. You may have heard of Peruvian corn beer, *chicha*. The starch-chopping enzymes in this case are found in human saliva, so the corn is chewed into small mushy cakes that are then left in the sun so the enzymes can do their work. Gross? Maybe at first, but it's still sterile because the corn is boiled for at least an hour after that. In fact, nihonshu used to be made this way (*kuchikami saké* or "mouth-chewed alcohol") as were many varieties of alcohol around the globe. Shochu is similar in that it needs a little help in converting starch into sugar. However, malted grains aren't allowed in the production of shochu, and neither is spitting—figurative blood, sweat, and tears maybe, but definitely no saliva.

Malting and chewing are replaced by a starch and mold mixture called *kōji*. We're discussing the production of potato shochu here, but more often than not potato shochu actually uses an entirely different base material to begin with: rice. The most common way to prepare 'rice *kōji*' is similar to the way they do it in the nihonshu world—*kōji kin* spores are sprinkled onto rice that has been washed, steamed, and then allowed to cool to about 35-40 degrees Celsius on a large table that has low, lined walls like a shallow pool. During the first dozen hours or so the rice is stirred regularly to make sure that the *kōji kin* has a chance to spread throughout the entire white, fluffy bed. A little more than half of a day later, this mixture is separated into rectangular wooden boxes (*kōji buta*), and these containers are carefully stacked in a checkerboard fashion so that the temperature of each small box of developing rice *kōji* can be closely monitored. The *kōji* is usually ready roughly 40-42 hours after the *kōji kin* spores first come in contact with the rice, and due to evaporation the grains of rice are quite hard at this point. While rice *kōji* is by far the most common type used to make shochu and awamori, barley *kōji* and sweet potato *kōji* are also popular with shochu consumers.

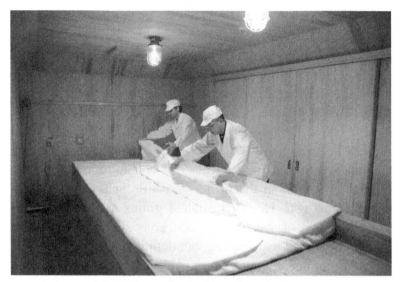

Covering a bed of handmade *kōji*.

Just to be clear, *kōji kin* are the mold spores, and *kōji* is rice (or another starch) that has *kōji kin* living on and inside of it. Please bear in mind that even though we're focusing on *kome* (rice) *kōji* in this chapter, *mugi* (barley), *imo* (potato), and *soba* (buckwheat) *kōji* are routine as well. Regardless of the base starch involved, it is crucial that the *kōji kin* is provided an advantageous environment to spread throughout the starch source. To that end, distilleries build insulated *kōji* rooms that carefully regulate temperature and humidity so that the *kōji kin* can run rampant. At this early stage, the *kōji kin* provide enzymes as they work their way into the grains of rice. The enzymes, specifically Alpha-amylase and amyloglucosidase, work together to chop the long starch chains into shorter chunks and convert them into glucose. Glucose is basically just fuel when it comes to making shochu and awamori, so when the yeast is added during the next step of this process, it's going to go bonkers at the biggest buffet of its life.

There are currently three main types of *kōji kin* used in *kōji* preparation. Listed from most to least commonly used in the shochu industry, the three types are white, black, and yellow *kōji kin*. Both white and black *kōji kin* are valued for the citric acid that they create in the mash (*moromi*), an essential defense against airborne bacteria and other nasties that can seriously foul up the delicate fermentation process, especially during the first couple of days. This is an even more pressing concern considering the hot and humid climate of the main production centers for shochu and awamori, so the citric acid is key. In most instances, white *kōji kin* can be counted on to soften and round the ingredients it touches. Black *kōji kin*, on the other hand, is loved for how it separates and highlights the flavors in the mash and adds impact to the final product. Many times you'll notice a light sweetness and more memorable finish in shochu made with black *kōji kin*.

Yellow *kōji kin*, the type used to make most nihonshu, has found its way into some shochu distilleries even though it's not a big fan of the hot and humid climate of southern Kyushu. Fortunately, advanced technology has made it much easier to control the temperatures within brewing and distilling facilities, so shochu consumers are able to enjoy an increasing number of labels that employ yellow *kōji kin* for help with fermentation. This type of mold affords a lighter and fruitier treatment of the mash constituents. However, as yellow *kōji kin* doesn't produce citric acid like its white and black counterparts, distilleries must be exceedingly careful with their temperature management to prevent mash infection by wild yeast. When everything goes to plan, the result is fruit and flowers on the nose, and a *prettier* treatment of the other mash constituents.

This *kōji* is ready for the first fermentation.

Whatever the color, distilleries typically purchase *kōji kin* from specialty suppliers. The traditional method of *kōji* preparation described here used to be done completely by hand, but many distilleries have automated parts of the process. For example, it is incredibly common for bigger distilleries to use large metal drums or conveyor belts to expedite rice steaming. Others have made *kōji* preparation less time-consuming by opting for far larger boxes than the small and labor-intensive trays that were once the only way to go in the shochu world. Also, please keep in mind that the specifics of everything in this chapter can vary wildly according to the instincts and methods of the *tōji* and the ambitions of the distillery.

2. First *moromi* fermentation (*ichiji shikomi*)
Once the *kōji kin* has completely spread throughout the rice, the *kōji* is ready. Water and yeast are mixed with it to create the mash. The *kōji* is flush with glucose, so the yeast can quickly get to work creating alcohol. Depending on the size of the distillery,

this starter fermentation will take place either in earthenware pots, often buried up to their necks in the distillery floor to help stabilize the temperature, or large metal vats. Most large-scale operations have opted for stainless steel because it's more economical in terms of maintenance and manpower. For every 100 kg of *kōji* loaded into the preferred fermentation vessel, generally about 120 liters of water and between 100-300 ml of yeast are added. This limited stage of fermentation helps the yeast get warmed up before the main ingredient is added in the next fermentation phase. The fermented mash (*moromi*) is stirred frequently and typically bubbles away for five to eight days.

The bubbling *moromi.*

As the first fermentation is winding down, workers elsewhere in the distillery are busy preparing the truckloads of freshly-harvested sweet potatoes (*imo*) that have just arrived. They are washed and then have any blemishes or bruises carved out of them. This is one part of the production process that can't be easily automated, and a large number of workers are generally required to lop the ends off of the spuds, clean them up, and remove damaged specimens from the conveyor belt. After the potatoes are relieved of their imperfections, they head to the steam drum for a nice, hot bath. The steamed potatoes are then transported to the shredder which chops the soggy spuds into small pieces that will be easier for the *kōji kin* and yeast to deal with in the second stage of fermentation.

Final spud inspection before steaming.

3. Second *moromi* fermentation (*niji shikomi*)

Now that the mold spores and yeast have been given a head start and multiplied enormously, they can easily handle the massive payload of crushed sweet potato that is added along with considerably more water. This is the second stage of fermentation, and most *imo* shochu distillers use roughly five times as much chopped potato as the amount of rice that was used to create the starter mash in the previous step. The formula can vary, of course, but this is generally how distilleries go about phasing in larger quantities of starch for the mold and yeast to mingle with. In large-scale distilleries the second stage of fermentation is then allowed to bubble away in large tanks for anywhere from eight to 10 days. In smaller outfits, the starter mash is divided amongst several pots before the extra water and potatoes are added.

It should be pointed out here that not all types of shochu follow this procedure in lock-step. Awamori, for example, uses only one stage of fermentation. Known as *zenkōji shikomi*, all of the *kōji*, water, and yeast are added to the fermentation vessel at the same time. In other words, awamori combines the two fermentation stages into one. Shochu used to be made this way as well, but these days two fermentation stages are used because of their ability to produce a healthy and vigorous ferment. However, this doesn't hold for all types of shochu. Brown sugar shochu often includes a third stage. The first two *moromi* fermentations are technically the same as other types of shochu with brown sugar being added during the *niji shikomi* stage. However, the second stage is essentially split in two. Brown sugar is added to the bubbling *moromi* on separate occasions resulting in a third stage.

4. Distillation (*jōryū*)
Distillers don't make shochu, they make *kōji*. Stills make shochu. Once fermentation has ceased, the distiller has a couple of choices for how to proceed. As you may have already guessed, this is yet another stage during which everything that is done to the shochu can have a drastic influence on the character of the final product. The now quiet mash is pumped into a still and this is where shochu is finally produced. Stills, of course, are amazingly complex instruments that enable the separation of components in a liquid. If 'honkaku' is what the distiller is planning to print on the label, then a pot still (often called an alembic in Europe) will be used to boil the finished

moromi in batches. There are various types of pot still in use, but the basic principles remain the same. At sea level pure alcohol (ethanol) boils at just under 78.4 degrees Celsius (172° F), so the resulting vapor will contain a stronger concentration of alcohol than the *moromi* that is being heated at the bottom of the pot. The alcohol vapors rise and are collected in the cone at the top before being fed into a cooling column where they recondense before dripping into a collection container. And *voila!* We have shochu.

A pot still at Satsuma Musou Distillery
in Kagoshima Prefecture.

If the distiller is aiming to make *kōrui* shochu, then a patent still will be used to create a distillate with as high a concentration of alcohol as possible. The first patent still was used in commercial alcohol production in Scotland in the early 1800's where Irishman Aeneas Coffey is credited with bringing this form of continuous distillation to the masses, and it found widespread adoption around the world over the next century. The patent still arrived in Japan in 1895, and *kōrui* shochu was born in 1910.

Unlike continuous distillation, where the alcohol undergoes several distillation cycles in order to maximize its purity, batch distillation results in many of the esters from the flora used in the mash (sweet potato in this case) escaping from the still along with the alcohol. Just as in the distillation of some kinds of whiskey and other spirits such as Calvados Pays D'Auge AOC (which must be run through a pot still twice by law), this is a highly desirable outcome as it lends the final product more character and complexity. If the distillate is sent back into the pot a second or third time, then the product gradually becomes separated from the ingredients that were used to create it. A neutral alcohol is certainly the goal of *kōrui* shochu, vodka, and soju production, but this is decidedly not the case where honkaku shochu is concerned.

A pot still will begin by producing an ester-rich distillate called *hanatare* that is generally around 70% ABV, but this number tapers off as the run continues. The last part of the run is called *suedare*. At this point the ABV has fallen all the way to about 10% and exudes an organic acid-based aroma that adds depth and complexity to the distillate. The resulting unprocessed alcohol, or *genshu*, generally has an ABV in the mid to upper thirties although higher is certainly not uncommon. Insert your nostrils in the vicinity of the distillate and you'll be treated to a bracing blend of oils, gases, and alcohol from the starches involved in the ferment. This raw bouquet is entirely due to the scientific and gut-level decisions made by the head distiller and the back-breaking work of everyone in the fields and distillery.

Obviously, the quality of the ingredients used during the *kōji* and *moromi* production stages have a profound effect on the taste of the final product because some of those flavors escape into the top of the still along with the vaporized alcohol. The rice *kōji*, sweet potato, yeast, and water all spent a considerable amount of time together before distillation, so it's only natural that you will notice the complex interplay between them when taking a sip. Honkaku shochu prizes these aromas and flavors, and distilleries across Japan have labored for generations to perfect the conditions and techniques necessary to create the ideal *moromi* for distillation.

Most *imo* shochu are distilled at atmospheric pressure (*jōatsu*), but another way that a distiller can shape the flavors of the final product is to use a more modern still, one that can reduce the pressure inside (*gen'atsu*). Essentially, this is distillation in a vacuum, and alcohol will therefore boil at a far lower temperature. While alcohol vapors will start to waft to the top of a regular pot still at just over 78 degrees Celsius, reducing the pressure will cause evaporation at anywhere from 40 to 60 degrees. This is obviously a much softer boil, and less of the *moromi* will escape with the vaporized alcohol. The result is a milder distillate where the influence of the other ingredients in the mash is softer. The relatively recent introduction of low pressure distilling has allowed the shochu industry to experiment with more refined flavors and reach a whole new segment of the market. Awamori distilleries in Okinawa have also begun experimenting with low pressure distillation—while once unheard of, it's becoming increasingly common to find awamori that blends distillate from the two types of pot still.

Inside the cooper's workshop.

5. Aging (*jukusei*)
Another major decision that distillers must negotiate is choosing the best conditions for aging the *genshu*. One could go the way of wine or whiskey and age shochu in a carefully crafted wooden barrel (*taru*). Larger distilleries will often opt for large stainless steel containers (*tanku*) for this purpose, while family-owned establishments may go with old-school

earthenware pots (*kame*). The choice here will bend the taste of the final product in a unique direction. I've seen long buildings lined up side by side at some distilleries with endless stacks of 450 liter casks. The most cavernous and mind-boggling that I've seen was at Kedogawa Shuzō in Kagoshima Prefecture, the makers of the internationally available and tasty Satsuma Shiranami line. The specifics are trade secrets, but they barrel-age their *mugi* shochu for a few years before bottling. Their Kannoko *mugi* develops a pseudo-whiskey coloration because of the barrel-aging, and the flavor is divine.

I'm a big fan of barrel-aged product, but earthenware pot-aged shochu is also delicious. Shochu is generally aged anywhere from one to three years, but it's still relatively rare for it to be stored much longer than that. It's often said that pot-aged shochu ages more quickly than whiskey thanks to the porous nature of the pots and the propensity for infrared rays to enter the vessel. At any rate, the rationale for aging shochu is the same as for other spirits; the harsher, brasher flavors will slowly diminish with time. These more aggressive flavors are released from shochu when gases separate from the liquid inside the conditioning vessel.

The large stainless steel tanks mentioned earlier are popular because they allow distilleries to age a massive volume of shochu at once. They also provide a highly stable environment for the aging process while imparting little to no extra flavors in the drink. Pot-aged shochu, on the other hand, often has a rounded or softened quality to it. This is attributed to the fact that air can permeate the small holes in the clay and interact with the sleeping shochu inside. If shochu is aged extensively in clay pots, it may be left with a light grey hue.

Conditioning tanks at Osuzuyama Distillery
in Miyazaki Prefecture.

Oak barrels, on the other hand, have a much stronger influence on the shochu resting inside. The charred wood slats used to make the barrels are responsible for the aromas and color that ease their way into the *genshu* along with complex changes to the flavor profile. However, caramel coloring is never added to honkaku shochu as it is to some varieties of whiskey. One of the many restrictions imposed on the industry is that distillers are obliged to keep their shochu within just a few shades of perfectly clear. In other words, you're not going to find a barrel-aged honkaku shochu that is darker than a light, golden straw color.

6. Before bottling
Dilution
Aged shochu undergoes a few more steps before finding its way into a bottle. The first step is blending (*burendo* or *chōgō*).

The contents of the aging vessels are usually mixed together to ensure consistency. After that, water is added (*warimizu*) to the shochu to bring the ABV down to the desired level for bottling. If the shochu is destined for those little plastic jars that they sell in convenience stores across Japan, then it might get diluted down to 20% ABV. If it's glass bottles and they're headed to California, then 24% ABV will often be the target. For the domestic market, 25% ABV is most common, but 30% or more is not at all out of the question.

Filtration
Filtration (*roka*) is a magnificently underrated part of the production process even though it's native to just about every brewing and distilling tradition out there. Generally employed either before or after the *warimizu* is added in another attempt to ensure consistency, filtration can be employed to further refine the flavor of the bottled product. The only caveat here is that white birch charcoal is not allowed at this stage; mass-produced vodka is known to use this medium in filtration, so its use is precluded in honkaku shochu production. However, other types of charcoal are acceptable, and filtration methods vary wildly in Japan as they do in the rest of the alcohol producing world.

Interestingly, the only time that you'll notice filtration mentioned on the label is when the contents *have not* been filtered at all (*muroka*). Bottles are proudly labeled *muroka* because it's a clear sign that the contents feature added character and depth. Depending on the substrate or method used, filtration is designed to remove impurities, off-flavors, chill haze, or color, so being able to say that a shochu is delicious even without filtration is certainly cause for some serious bragging. Indeed, *muroka* shochu are worth sampling wherever they may be found.

7. Bottling (*bin'dzume*)

After blending, dilution, and filtration, the shochu is pumped into the bottling machine where much of it will be sealed in 720 ml or 1800 ml bottles (*bin*) for the domestic market. The former is sometimes called a *yon gō bin* because it is four (*yon*) times the size of the *gō* decanters that are used to serve shochu and nihonshu in bars and restaurants. The 1.8 L (1.9 US quarts) bottles are called *isshō bin* and are a standard size in Japan. 10 times the size of a *gō* decanter, they are not ideal for home bars that lack space (like mine!). However, they look very impressive for special occasions, and in Japan they generally aren't as expensive as you might expect them to be.

The bottling setups are as varied as the distilleries themselves with smaller outfits employing a much more hands-on approach to everything from controlling the flow of shochu into the bottle to applying the labels. Larger companies, as you can probably imagine, have this process completely automated. The vast majority of honkaku shochu in Japan retails for between 800 and 2,000 yen (US$8-20) for a 720 ml bottle. The sturdy *isshō bin* tend to be priced between 1,800 yen and 4,000 yen making it very affordable for a spirit.

I've tried to keep this brief overview of shochu production as simple as possible while including enough detail to illustrate how the process is unique. It goes without saying, however, that the best way to get a solid grasp of the concepts outlined in this chapter is to actually visit a shochu distillery. If you're fortunate enough to be able to travel around Japan, try to include at least one distillery tour.

Chapter 4
Types of shochu

You have most likely seen them on the menu at nearly every alcohol-equipped establishment in Japan, mysterious cocktails that end in the syllable '*hai*'. And those *chūhai* drinks that seem to be the best bet at the convenience store in terms of easy-to-drink alcoholic content per hundred yen spent—is this shochu or vodka or what? But what of all these new bars that cater to shochu lovers—what are they drinking? Is it the same fuel that is powering these diverse parties, or are we talking about entirely different alcoholic animals here?

Quite simply, what we are dealing with is two varieties of the same drink that have different distillation processes and drinking purposes. At the risk of oversimplifying things just a bit, shochu, the alcohol distilled from a wide range of flora, can generally be divided into two main camps, honkaku and *kōrui*, and then one kind of fence-sitter, *konwa*.

The first half of this chapter is a quick-and-dirty introduction to the three major classifications of shochu. If this is something that you feel that you already have a handle on, skip forward to the ingredients section.

Honkaku Shochu
This book focuses, first and foremost, on honkaku shochu. Please don't forget that. When the word shochu is used on

its own, you can generally assume that I'm referring to the honkaku type. The same goes for when you visit a restaurant or bar and see shochu on the menu. The *kōrui* shochu that is mentioned in this chapter is not really worth writing a book about. It could be part of a book I suppose, a chapter maybe, but writing about *kōrui* shochu is about as enthralling as describing the intricacies of sliced white bread. It's important for combining with countless other ingredients to create highly pleasing end products, but on its own? No, I'd rather drink and write about something else, thank you.

Honkaku shochu (sometimes called *otsurui* shochu) is single-distilled, and full of flavor and aroma. To a far greater degree than the *kōrui* shochu detailed later in this chapter, it's the spirit that is finding new fans outside of Japan. People love it for its complexity and variety, and it's the closest thing Japan has to how shochu was originally made hundreds of years ago. 'Honkaku' can be translated as premium, authentic, or genuine, but it wasn't always called that. In an effort to help consumers distinguish which type of shochu was premium after the birth of *kōrui* shochu in 1910, the honkaku designation was added to the shochu lexicon in 1971. The word honkaku can only be printed on bottles that contain single-distilled shochu using official shochu ingredients and their *kōji* as designated by Japan's tax authorities. The most common raw ingredients, as we have learned, are sweet potato, barley, rice, brown sugar, and buckwheat.

Honkaku shochu makes up the bulk of what all of those new-fangled shochu bars in Tokyo are serving. Even chain izakaya around Japan tend to have at least half a dozen labels on their menus because they boast high cost performance and can be paired flexibly with food. Honkaku shochu is typically enjoyed neat, on the rocks, or with either hot or cool water. It is most frequently bottled at 25% ABV, but legally it can climb as high as 45% ABV. Honkaku shochu, the pride of the prefectures of Kyushu Island, is generally associated with southern parts of the archipelago.

Kōrui Shochu
Kōrui shochu, on the other hand, is produced primarily from sugar cane (molasses) and corn pretty much all over Japan. As you will remember from the discussion of Korean soju production in chapter two, *kōrui* shochu distilleries can minimize the labor-intensive *kōji* preparation process because fermentable sugars are much easier to come by in the mash ingredients, many of which are not allowed in honkaku shochu production. Tapioca, sugar beet, barley, and rice are also used as starch sources for this type of shochu. For the most part, *kōrui* is what's providing the kick in many of those restaurant cocktails and canned drinks that sparkle in supermarket and convenience store coolers in Japan. The distillate is repeatedly cycled through a patent still until it loses nearly all of its flavor profile and reaches 96% ABV. There is not a whole lot

happening on the nose either—this stuff (sometimes compared with vodka or soju) is ideal for cocktails and is generally the '*chū*' half of a canned '*chūhai*' (a drink containing shochu, soda, and a sweet or sour mixer of some sort). *Chūhai*, by the way, is a reduction of 'sho*chu high*ball', and the most common mixers used in restaurants are currently tea (oolong), grapefruit juice, or lemon juice.

Undiluted *kōrui* shochu is also added to some grades of nihonshu, such *as honjōzō*, in order to tame some of the more robust natural flavors that are produced during the brewing process, and this specially-ordered neutral spirit is referred to as 'brewer's alcohol' (*jōzō arukōru*). The maximum permissible ABV for *kōrui* shochu available to the general public, however, is 35%. While a small amount of undiluted *kōrui* shochu is blended into premium nihonshu to help calm it down, so to speak, or even to preserve the aromas in the mash, far larger volumes are added to vats of cheaper product in order to increase yields. Some types of pseudo-beer, an annoyingly popular class of canned beverage in Japan, are also fortified with brewer's alcohol.

Another popular drink, *umeshu*, also uses *kōrui* shochu as its base, as do a plethora of homemade fruit, spice and vegetable-infused liqueurs. *Kōrui* shochu is a major part of the overall shochu market and has only recently seen its ubiquity infringed upon by the whiskey highball craze that came into full force in 2010-11. *Kōrui* shochu features quite a bit more in the second half of this book where homemade liqueurs and cocktail recipes are provided for your experimentation (see chapter nine).

Perhaps the easiest way to tell the difference when shochu shopping in Japan is that honkaku is most often found in 720 ml or larger glass bottles (although it also can be purchased in large cartons). *Kōrui*, on the other hand, is most commonly packaged in gigantic, clear, plastic jugs. Imbibe with caution.

As a general rule, just don't purchase anything that has "甲類" (*kōrui*) printed anywhere on the front label. To be fair, even if you call a metropolis such as Paris, New York, or Sydney home, I don't anticipate those large jugs showing up in a bottle shop near you anytime soon, but when traveling around Japan, then it's perhaps wise to keep this old adage in mind, "Bigger is not always better."

Konwa Shochu

Konwa shochu is a blend of the two categories detailed above, *kōrui* and *otsurui*. In an effort to reach the portion of the population that would happily sip honkaku shochu were it not for some of its more vibrant qualities, the industry created a new category that attempts to mix the best of both worlds. This is a little bit like blended scotch, minus the use of such a wide variety of liquid constituents (Johnnie Walker Red Label, for example, blends more than 30 whiskies). The result is a tamer shochu that some find more to their liking.

    Konwa shochu is divided into two sub-groups, and everything must be clearly labeled so that consumers don't accidentally buy *konwa* when they intend to purchase honkaku (*konwa* shochu labeling regulations were most recently amended on January 1st, 2005). The first subdivision of *konwa* shochu uses 49% or less *otsurui* shochu with the rest being filled out by *kōrui*. You will know that single-distilled shochu is in the minority if you can find 焼酎甲類乙類混和 (shochu ***kōrui otsurui** konwa*) somewhere on the label. The fact that *kōrui* is listed before *otsurui* is the main indicator of what you're purchasing. In practice, it is quite common for the percentage of *otsurui* shochu to make up less than 30% of the bottle's contents. The more *kōrui* involved in the blend, obviously, the milder the product will taste, and the greater the potential profit margin for the producer.

The second group, as is probably already obvious, contains everything sporting a majority of the good stuff. If the distillery uses at least 51% *otsurui* shochu in the blend, then they can reverse the *kōrui* and *otsurui* on the label (shochu *otsurui kōrui konwa*). This will result in a mix with relatively more character although it should still be a bit cheaper than most bottles of honkaku shochu.

One confusing thing about *konwa* shochu is that it is packaged in the same size containers, both glass and carton, as honkaku. Just keep your eyes peeled for the word 混和 (*konwa*) somewhere on the package. The shochu industry has made significant efforts over the past decade to help consumers avoid accidentally buying *konwa* shochu when searching for honkaku. As a result of these adjustments, the labels currently in use are much easier to navigate than their former selves.

Ingredients

Now that we have a basic understanding of the different shochu classifications that have been established by the Japan Tax Office, let us now turn to the major ingredients that are used in the production of honkaku shochu. As mentioned earlier, there are more than 50 core ingredients that are currently permitted for use in its production, but we'll stick to the heavy hitters, namely potato, barley, rice, brown sugar, and buckwheat.

Potato (*imo*)

There are dozens of sweet potato varietals being used in shochu production today, and many more are currently in the pipelines as distilleries cross-breed different types to create taters with a higher starch content and excellent taste in the finished product. The spuds used to make *imo* shochu are usually sweet potatoes, now known in Japan as *satsuma imo*. But the humble potato had to travel a long way in order to finally hit it big in Kyushu. The tuber has its roots in the Andes of South

America, and Spanish explorer Francisco Pizarro is credited with being the first to export the starchy vegetable outside of the southern continent. Within several decades potatoes had quite literally travelled around the world and are now in the top five of the most important world staple crops according to the Smithsonian.

Planting sweet potatoes.

Pizarro isn't directly responsible for the sweet potato's eventual journey to Japan, but other traders eventually brought it with them to China, and from there they were shipped to the Ryūkyū Islands in 1605 by a government trade official who would be recorded in history as Noguni Sōkan. Nobody knows his birth name, so he's remembered affectionately by his job title, and crucially he wasted no time planting the unglamorous yet nutritious plant in his hometown of Kadena. 100 years later, Riemon Maeda carried sweet potatoes north to Kagoshima (then called Satsuma) where local officials were highly enthused by how easily they grew in the area's volcanic ash-laced soil. Indeed, barley and rice didn't grow quite so happily in Kagoshima, and after some cajoling by the government not all that dissimilar to what had taken place in Europe a century and a half earlier, many farmers began to switch over to this foreign crop. Now sweet potatoes are harvested all over Japan with the major areas of production residing in Kagoshima, Ibaraki, Chiba, and Miyazaki Prefectures.

Kagoshima is the undisputed champ of *satsuma imo*, however, producing over 40% of the domestic supply on a yearly basis. The citizens of Kagoshima also set the national standard in honkaku versus *kōrui* consumption—the former makes up over 97% of all the shochu that Kagoshimans enjoy annually. In comparison, while Tokyo residents combine to drink three times as much shochu on a yearly basis thanks to a massive population advantage, just 41% of the total is honkaku. City folk like their cocktails, I guess.

The following are a few of the most commonly used sweet potato varietals used to make shochu:

- *koganesengan*: Where *imo* shochu is concerned, *koganesengan* is currently top dog. While not on the same level as rice, this spud is known for having a relatively high starch content, a sweet taste that is also used in cooking, and many people remark that they can smell chestnuts in the final product. One drawback with *koganesengan* is that it doesn't keep very long so the potatoes have to be rushed to the distillery soon after being dug out of the ground.

- *joy white*: The Kyushu Okinawa Agriculture Research Center made an important contribution to the shochu world in 1994 with this varietal. It's known as the first sweet potato to be bred specifically with shochu production in mind, and as its moniker implies, the pulp is very white. It sports a decent starch count but imparts a milder, balanced flavor into the shochu that is often described as being fruity.

- *beni hayato*: You can be excused for remarking that this delicious type of potato looks a bit like a carrot because it actually carries a decent helping of beta-carotene. You'll likely sense a bit of carrot in the nose of shochu made with *beni hayato* potatoes—its sweetness keeping it relevant even though it doesn't pack an impressive starch punch.

Other commonly used sweet potato varietals include more *benis*, specifically *beni satsuma* and *beni azuma*, plus other usual suspects such as *shiro yutaka*, *daichi no yume*, and the recently introduced *toki masari* which was a 2007 creation by the same brilliant folks that gave the world *joy white* sweet potatoes. Just as the type of malt in beer or grape varietal in wine has a profound effect on the final product, the type of potato that is dropped into the pots during the second stage of fermentation has everything to do with what you smell and taste in your glass. In addition to the types of potato listed above, there are about three dozen more that are currently used to make shochu.

Now let's take a look at what goes into making some of the other popular types of shochu, including the long-loved barley shochu that really found its footing in the 1970s and '80s.

Barley (*mugi*)
Humans largely stopped their wandering ways many millennia ago because they figured out how to domesticate the growth of barley, make bread, and most importantly, brew beer. Barley has more recently featured heavily in the production of spirits all around the world including malt and grain whiskey, vodka, and gin. The shochu industry uses two-row barley which grows

best in cooler climates, and currently Australia is the leading provider of imported barley for the Japanese shochu market.

A barley field in Miyazaki Prefecture.

However, many distilleries, such as Kuroki Honten in Miyazaki Prefecture, are starting to differentiate themselves by using domestic barley in their products. Kuroki Honten has for years grown its own barley on-site for use in its legendary line of shochu. Two-row barley is preferable to its six-row cousin because its large kernels have a high starch content and lower enzyme (protein) count, and the domestic harvesting season is typically April-May. Barley grains are generally polished (*seibaku*) down to 60-65% of their original size before use.

Rice (*kome*)

As discussed in chapter three, rice is a major player in the world of shochu production. It is the only starch used in the production of awamori and *kasutori* shochu (made from nihonshu lees), and it is the majority stakeholder in the world of rice shochu. Many other varieties rely on it for *kōji* production, and in the case of brown sugar shochu, its use is required during fermentation. Rice softens and rounds the final product when used in *kōji* preparation.

The types of rice used to make shochu can broadly be grouped into two families, *japonica* and *indica*, both of which contain hundreds of strains. The differences between the two groups is mainly one of region; *japonica* rice is primarily grown in more temperate climates such as Japan, parts of China, and even Australia. *Indica* strains tend to grow best in relatively tropical climates, and as you may have guessed, this includes southern China, Thailand, India, and even some parts of the United States. *Japonica* rice is shorter and chubbier than *indica*, and it's sticky when cooked. *Indica*, on the other hand, has a fluffy quality because the individual grains aren't as sticky and tend to separate from each other after boiling.

Awamori, as a rule, only uses *indica* rice, and this is sometimes expressed as *Thai-mai* (タイ米: rice from Thailand) on the label. This long, thin varietal of rice doesn't absorb water quite as easily as *japonica* rice does, and it can be quite brittle during the polishing process. This means that the grains routinely crack and break, but the silver lining here is that the rice grains absorb water more easily during the steaming process that way. Incidentally, the faint vanilla notes in some awamori is thought to come from the hundreds of kilos of *indica* rice used during the fermentation process.

Indica is sometimes used for rice *kōji* production in honkaku shochu production as well. Depending on the style of shochu being made, distillers may be free to use either *indica* or *japonica* rice for *kōji* preparation. However, there is currently a trend toward using domestically produced grains in the shochu industry as consumers are beginning to look for evidence on the label of locally grown rice. Therefore, it is unlikely that *japonica* rice *kōji* will wane in popularity.

The many distillers that use *japonica* rice often use strains that are mainstays in the nihonshu industry as well. *Hinohikari* and *nipponbare* are two such rice varietals that enjoy widespread use in both sectors of the Japanese drinks industry. One big difference here is the extent to which the rice is polished before it's steamed. In nihonshu production, the amount of polishing is directly related to the grade of the product and its price tag. The more polishing, the higher the grade. Therefore, a nihonshu with a rice polishing ratio (*seimaibuai*) of 55%, meaning that 45% of each grain of rice has been milled away, will likely be more expensive than one with a ratio of 70%. Shochu distilleries don't need to worry about these graded limitations on the rice that they use, so most shochu rice is polished lightly to 85-90% of its original size. The only major concern for distillers is that the rice tastes good, and that they can draw the umami out of the grains during fermentation.

Brown sugar (*kokutō*)

It's said that sugar cane first reached Amami Guntō, a southern clutch of islands that are part of Kagoshima Prefecture, from China in 1610 before spreading to Okinawa, but it wasn't until after Christmas day, 1953, when America returned the islands to Japanese control that this regional variety of 'island saké' finally joined the honkaku shochu club. Importantly, *kokutō* shochu must be made with rice *kōji* in order to differentiate it from rum. The brown sugar used to make Amami's famous *kokutō* shochu is sourced from the Amami Islands, Okinawa, and sometimes even from overseas. Brown sugar is graded according to color and texture in many parts of the world, and in Japan there are five grades. From best to worst, the grades in Japan are Special, First Class, Second Class, Third Class, and everything else. Distillers in the Amami Islands use only Special and First Class brown sugar in their shochu. For every 100 kg of sugar cane, about 10 kg of brown sugar can be produced.

Buckwheat (*soba*)

The first *soba* shochu, Unkai, was produced in 1973 by Unkai Shuzō in Miyazaki Prefecture. It's a mild and easy-sipping shochu that has gained wide popularity in Japan. It is often served in *soba* noodle restaurants, and mixing it with the leftover *soba*-flavored soup in your bowl after the noodles are gone is a pleasant way to enjoy it. The smoothness of the drink, however, belies how difficult it is to produce shochu from buckwheat. The husks are quite hard and must be removed before the kernels are coarsely crushed and steeped. The main challenge in using buckwheat is it's a little too good at holding onto moisture which impedes healthy *kōji* preparation. Therefore, Unkai's revolutionary product uses barley *kōji* instead. It wasn't until 2004 that Takara Shuzō figured out how to make *soba kōji*, and the result was the world's first 100% *soba* shochu, Towari.

Chapter 5
Reading the label

The ornate calligraphy on shochu bottle labels in Japan can be at once beautiful and infuriatingly difficult to decipher. At times, it can seem like the "artist" responsible for smearing the ink on the label was hoping to create a riddle for even the most accomplished of *kanji* readers. To wit, much like when dealing with the obscure *kanji* used on nihonshu labels, many people fluent in Japanese will be forced to offer two or more possible pronunciations for the brand when asked to interpret what is stamped on the bottle.

This is not meant to belittle the art of calligraphy (*shodō*) in any way, shape, or form. Nor is it an indication that a novice should simply give up on their quest to figure out the name of what they're drinking or thinking of purchasing. There is a wealth of helpful information on most labels, and one of those is often a furigana translation of the drink's name. Some brands will even include a Romanized transliteration of the name on the label. Indeed, shochu producers are now translating nearly all of the information on bottles destined for sale internationally, so the act of reading labels overseas is usually not as difficult as what you'll encounter in Japan.

The name of the shochu will certainly be listed, as will the main ingredients used in the mash. ABV will also be listed, and you'll probably find that honkaku shochu bottled for export is sometimes a percentage point or two lower than in Japan. Finally, the name of the distillery and possibly even the city of origin will be listed on the front.

One thing that you will still sometimes see on the label that you should ignore is the word 'soju,' Korean-made clear liquor. Soju is somewhat similar to *kōrui* shochu although it's often a bit sweeter. As explained in the second chapter of this book, the shochu industry continues to print this on its labels in America so that it can be sold by establishments that have a beer and wine permit rather than a full-blown liquor license (depending on the state). Hopefully the tax laws will eventually be amended to prevent this mislabeling from continuing, but I'm not holding my breath.

You'll never find the word 'soju' written anywhere on a bottle of honkaku shochu in Japan, trust me. But aside from the obvious language differences, a lot of the other information on the label is actually quite similar to what you'll find on the front of a shochu bottle in Japan. If there's a back label, then you'll likely be treated to a blurb telling you a bit about the region where it was made, and maybe even a summary of the distillery's history. The information about ingredients will all be there as well, including an indication of what type of *kōji* was used. It is very common these days for distillers to proudly display the kanji for black (黒: pronounced *kuro*) when that was the type of mold employed in the *kōji*. Many times the word *kuro* will be added as a prefix or suffix to the name of the shochu itself. Skip forward to chapter eight for a few examples of this.

Tax and labeling laws in Japan dictate that a number of other shochu classifications can be claimed in addition to the basics mentioned earlier. There are four WTO-protected regional appellations that can be added to the label if the product is true to type and made in one of those locales. This is just like the location-specific protections granted to drinks like champagne and Scotch whiskey. Satsuma (薩摩) is used for potato shochu from Kagoshima Prefecture, Iki (壱岐) for barley shochu made on one island of Nagasaki Prefecture, Kuma (球磨) for rice shochu made in southern Kumamoto Prefecture, and Ryūkyū (琉球) is the geographical indication reserved for awamori produced in Okinawa. If you're looking for one of these famous appellations, then you're seeking the time-honored representatives of the shochu world.

Satsuma Shochu (Kagoshima Prefecture)

"Satsuma" is the former name for the region that is now known as Kagoshima Prefecture. In order for a distillery to be able to print the WTO-protected Satsuma Shochu designation on the label, the product must be completely sourced and produced in Satsuma. This means that all of the potatoes must be from Satsuma, and the water must be drawn from the region as well.

SATSUMA SHOCHU

Satsuma Shochu logo.

Furthermore, only rice or sweet potato *kōji* can be used during fermentation, and the entire production, both pre- and post-distillation, must take place in Kagoshima Prefecture. While potato shochu produced on peripheral islands situated within roughly 100 km of the Kagoshima mainland can qualify for Satsuma Shochu status, *imo* shochu distilled on the Amami Islands cannot use this designation.

Iki Shochu (Iki Island, Nagasaki Prefecture)

There are currently seven distilleries on this small cluster of islands (just over 130 square kilometers in total land mass) that are producing Iki Shochu, a complex *mugi* that is one part rice and two parts barley. Iki Island is thought to be the birthplace of *mugi* shochu in Japan thanks to its trading connections with the Korean Peninsula several hundred years ago. Although the island is now famous for *mugi* shochu, *kasutori* shochu

Iki Shochu logo.

was initially more common. Rice shortages and government taxation policy took a toll on the region's nihonshu and *kasutori* shochu producers, and *mugi* shochu gradually took over. Iki Shochu is prized for its unique sweetness and depth when compared with shochu made from a 100% barley mash.

Kuma Shochu logo.

Kuma Shochu (Kuma Region, Kumamoto Prefecture)

Kuma Shochu is distilled in the Hitoyoshi Basin from a 100% rice mash that uses water from the local Kuma River. The river is recognized as one of the three fastest flowing in the country, and there are currently 28 distilleries in the region that make official Kuma Shochu by sourcing water from its subterranean stream. Thanks to the regional climate and fresh water supply, Kuma is famous for rice production, and the quality in the fields translates directly to the bottle. Kuma distillers have increased their use of low pressure (*gen'atsu*) distillation over the past few decades to increase the spectrum of flavor and aroma that can be enjoyed in these tasty shochu.

Ryūkyū Awamori (Okinawa Prefecture)

Okinawa was the first place in Japan where distilled spirits were produced, and the shochu industry can trace its roots back to the traditions that took hold nearly six centuries ago. Awamori has been creating fast friends ever since, and there are now roughly four dozen distilleries on this wide-stretched archipelago that make the geographically protected drink. Awamori bearing the Ryūkyū banner must be locally produced and adhere to all of the normal awamori rules governing the ingredients, fermentation method (*zenkōji shikomi*), and

Ryūkyū Awamori logo.

pot still distillation. Aging is an essential part of the awamori production process, and fractional blending is common throughout the industry.

Aged shochu

Some distilleries choose to age their shochu for more than three years. This practice is becoming increasingly common, and the trend is likely to continue as the various players in the industry clamber for ways to add value to their range of products. Shochu that has been aged for at least 36 months, and still makes up at least 50% of the product after blending, is permitted to advertise this fact by printing *chōki chozō* (長期 貯蔵) on the label. Another aging-related designation that can be found on some labels is *kashidaru chozō* (樫樽 貯蔵) which means that the spirit contained within spent some time in an oak barrel before bottling.

Awamori has an aging tradition that is far more developed than that found in the shochu industry, and there is a whole range of technicalities and labeling intricacies to go along with it. The most important word to know is *koshu* (古酒), pronounced *kūsu* in Okinawa, and it indicates that more than half of the liquid volume was aged for at least three years. It is also helpful to know the kanji for year (年: pronounced *nen*) since it will help you figure out the age of the bottled contents. Awamori that is a blend of 70% five year *koshu* and 30% eight year *koshu* will display something like this on the back label: 5年古酒 70% ・ 8年古酒 30%. On the front label, however, the claim will be that the contents were aged for five years; the younger of the two numbers is the official printed age of the awamori. You should be able to find a 'born on' date somewhere on the bottle as well.

Another intriguing layer of the awamori aging process is what's known as fractional blending. This is basically the same as what happens in a Solera setup where the year's vintage is put in a large aging container annually. After a number of years, let's say six, the oldest container is partially tapped and bottled, and the containers are cascaded from younger to older. In other words, the oldest container is refilled with product from the second oldest vessel, which is in turn reimbursed with distillate from the third. This continues all the way through the Solera. After alcohol from the sixth aging container has been used to refill the fifth, the current year's product (*shinshu*) is added to the youngest vessel. Soleras are commonly used to make things like vinegar and sherry, and they can achieve impressive results when spirits are involved. In fact, distillers of Spanish brandy are required by law to use a Solera before bottling. The results speak for themselves. Much of the roundness and smoothness of aged awamori can be attributed to this traditional system of fractional blending.

Genshu

The word *genshu* (原酒) on the label means that nothing has been added to the drink since it was collected from the still. This indicates that the drink has not been diluted, and the rule for *genshu* is that they are no weaker than 36% ABV. The highest they are allowed to go while maintaining their status as honkaku shochu is 45%. You may also find *te'dzukuri* (手造り) printed on the label, and this signifies that the *kōji* was made in the traditional style, by hand.

The E Mark logo is ubiquitous across Japan.

There are a few logos that have been cooked up by regional distilling associations to help provide further stamps of quality on the bottle. The "E Mark" is used across the country to signal products that are sourced locally, and in Kagoshima Prefecture this logo can be found on the back label of product that was distilled using Kagoshima-sourced sweet potatoes and rice. If you're curious about what they mean, the three E's arranged in a pyramid stand for "Excellent Quality," "Exact Expression," and "Harmony with Ecology."

Kagoshima's shochu industry has actually come up with several other bottle badges over the past decade, including the Satsuma Shochu kettle silhouette that was born in 2007. The Amami Islands, famous for their brown sugar shochu, have an Amami *Kokutō* Shochu (奄美黒糖焼酎) logo, and even Nagano Prefecture, not exactly a hotbed of shochu activity yet, has found it advantageous to allow producers to stamp bottles with a circular chunk of text showing that the ingredients are local.

Amami Kokutō Shochu logo

It is very likely that more regional designations and logos will be developed as the localvore movement continues to grow.

Chapter 6
How to serve shochu

Serving shochu

Now that we've gone through all the basics, it's time to sit down and get serious. If you don't already have a bottle of honkaku shochu in the house, go get one. If you happen to live or be in a part of the world that doesn't have a ready supply (admittedly, unless you're in a major city, you may be out of luck), then either make a phone call or plan a visit to your local bottle shop. They need to be made aware that they can profit from selling shochu.

Let's think about all the different ways that shochu can be enjoyed. There aren't many other drinks on the planet that have a comparable amount of flexibility in terms of how they are commonly consumed. The time of year, region, variety of shochu and accompanying cuisine can all have an influence on how it is served. By and large, of course, the best way to serve it will come down to the simple question of personal taste.

For obvious reasons, the fastest way to prepare a glass of shochu is to serve it neat. A couple of shots should do. Most shochu weigh in at about 25% ABV, so it won't go to your head quite as quickly as a single malt whiskey, but as always moderate consumption is advised—don't go filling your coffee tumbler to the brim with shochu.

It's also worth experimenting with chilling the bottle that you plan to drink. This is, of course, not done in an effort to make the contents keep longer. Shochu is a distilled beverage and will not sour or spoil after opening if stored properly. The merits of refrigeration are to avoid diluting the drink with ice and to see how the spices, sweetness, and earthy notes reveal themselves as the drinking vessel is gradually warmed by your hand. Higher ABV shochu, such as *hanatare*, are sometimes stored in the freezer and then enjoyed ice cold. In fact, one of the most memorable and delicious culinary experiences I've had occurred while visiting distilleries in Miyazaki Prefecture. The host of the dinner advised us to pour a puddle of icy *hanatare* into the half-shell raw oysters in front of us, and it was divine! Go ahead and pop that bottle in the freezer right next to the Bombay Sapphire. You can thank me later.

Another delightful way to experience shochu is to drink it on the rocks. Just add ice cubes to a Collins glass or small tumbler, pour your shochu of choice over the top, and sip slowly. There are many bartenders in Tokyo and elsewhere who claim that the size and shape of the cubes used can affect the taste of the drink. These are generally the same places that plop ice balls or large bergs in their drinks. The best argument in favor of this serving style is that larger chunks of ice melt more slowly than cubes. Naturally, this means that your drink will become watered down less quickly and retain something similar to its first sip flavor longer. I'm not aware of a freezer equipped with an automatic ice ball maker, so if this is something you'd like to try with your shochu, then you'll need to either pick up some silicone ice ball molds or become handy with an ice pick. Regular ice cubes work just fine for me, especially since freezer space is limited in my household, and I've never been accused of being a slow consumer of shochu. Whichever way you decide to go, I advise making ice with bottled or mineral water. This is especially necessary if you live in an urban setting and are dependent on the city's hyper-treated water supply.

Shochu is often cut with water and this serving style is called *mizuwari* in Japanese. This can be a good way to dilute the alcohol in the shochu or even to mute the stronger flavors that might overpower the taste buds if consumed straight. Pour the shochu first, and then slowly add mineral water. If poured smoothly, you shouldn't need to mix it because the liquids will mingle automatically. The ratio of shochu to water can vary according to a variety of factors. If we look to the prefectures of shochu's origin for guidance, a plethora of drinking preferences are evident. In Oita Prefecture, for example, barley shochu is commonly mixed 3:7 (shochu to water). This is very different from the somewhat standard ratio of *roku yon* (6:4) and too weak for my personal tastes, but in all fairness I'm pretty sure that they are counting the ice cubes in the seven parts of prescribed water. You may find that *mizuwari* shochu is served with ice in many places, but I recommend ditching the cubes when serving drinks at home. Rather than watering your shochu down further with melting ice, why not just chill the bottle and water in the fridge for a few hours? If you really like the idea of rocks in your drink, then it is perhaps better to add less water and more shochu. After all, shochu on the rocks eventually becomes *mizuwari* if you take your time enjoying it.

By the way, a quick word on the ratios commonly used for water-cut shochu in Japan. You may be wondering why it is 6:4 and not 3:2. There are several reasons that I can think of, the least of which is the fact that it allows easily calculable precision when ordering drinks. Both sides of the ratio should always add up to 10. It's a little bit easier to negotiate the constituents of a drink broken into tenths than to bounce back and forth between thirds, quarters, and fifths. This is especially true when introducing a friend to shochu, and you'd like to order a weaker potato shochu *mizuwari* for the first round. Another nice thing about breaking a drink down this way is that it's also relatively easy to calculate the alcohol content. A 25% ABV shochu that is cut 9:1 with water will logically experience a 2.5% reduction in alcohol content. Therefore, a 6:4 *mizuwari* has an alcohol content similar to that of nihonshu at 15%, and a 5:5 is in wine territory at 12.5%.

When drinking awamori, which is generally higher in ABV than its shochu cousin, *mizuwari* is recommended and is indeed the most common drinking style in Okinawa. The awamori to water ratio is largely up to you, but I recommend the *roku yon* formula mentioned above, especially if you're new to awamori. Feel free to change the quantities to your own liking though. Every shochu and awamori will deserve its own specific treatment—my only advice is that you don't absolutely drown the drink with water as it'll dull what makes it unique and enjoyable.

One of the most popular ways to drink shochu when the mercury drops is with hot water, or *oyuwari*. Hot water can help let the bouquet of aromas from the shochu waft into the air for you to get a better whiff. Just like preparing a glass of shochu *mizuwari*, there is a proper way to prepare an *oyuwari* drink. Establishments that take their shochu seriously will generally heat the water until it gets in the ballpark of 70-80 degrees Celsius (158 degrees Fahrenheit), but don't hesitate to experiment with what works best and is easiest with the shochu that you have on hand. Factors such as the temperature of the cup and shochu will drop the heat in the overall mix to somewhere between 40 and 50 degrees Celsius. You'll also notice that, counter-intuitively perhaps, the hot water is added to the cup first in an *oyuwari*. One reason for adding the alcohol last is that the difference in temperature and gravity will cause the two ingredients to mix automatically. Another reason for adding the hot water first is that the drink will cool more slowly than if you add the room temperature shochu first. Personally, I like my *oyuwari* piping hot, so I add boiled water to a kilned shochu cup and it quickly cools to around 85-90 degrees. After adding my shochu of choice, I have the perfect answer for a cold January night.

If you have a cooking thermometer handy, then it's possible to get supremely nerdy and pinpoint a desired serving temperature for your *oyuwari*. Assuming that the room temperature of the shochu is 24 degrees Celsius, and we plan to use the standard 6:4 ratio, let's use the following step-by-step equation to arrive at a 45 degree *oyuwari* mix. Take the target temperature for your drink and multiply it by 10 (45 X 10 = 450). Then multiply the temperature of the shochu by its ratio equivalent in the *oyuwari* mix (24 X 6 = 144). Subtract the second number from the first (450 - 144 = 306), and then divide by the hot water's ratio in the mix (306 / 4 = 76.5). That result, 76.5, is the temperature in degrees Celsius that the water needs to be heated to before mixing with the room temperature shochu.

While we're on the topic of high temperatures, it is not unheard of to drink shochu *atsukan*, a preparation method that is probably more common with nihonshu. *Atsukan* involves heating the shochu itself rather than adding hot water to it. Some people also enjoy *atsukan* shochu poured over ice—the shochu presents a different flavor profile after it's been heated and cooled rapidly.

One of my favorite places to drink shochu in Tokyo is well-known for its *nurukan* (*oyuwari* that's not quite so hot—about 40 degrees Celsius). The intriguing part is that the owner of the bar gauges the temperature of the water while it's being heated by putting his hand on the side of the metal cup. He then mixes the warm water and shochu, and I really enjoy drinking potato and rice shochu this way. The hot water brings out the earthiness and sweetness in both the aroma and flavor. But much like shochu prepared *mizuwari*, there are some regional preferences that often influence how much hot water is used and what temperature it's heated to. People in Kagoshima tend to prefer their *oyuwari* served at around 45 degrees Celsius, but the ratio employed will depend on the importance of the bouquet when drinking. The good people of Kumamoto Prefecture, home of the Kuma Shochu appellation, naturally have a strong affinity for rice shochu, and the standard 6:4 mix is generally served at a lower temperature, often around 40 degrees. Meanwhile, up in northern Kyushu, barley and rice shochu are served *oyuwari* when the mercury recedes. Importantly, all of these massive generalizations highlight the fact that people in shochu's homeland are just as particular about their shochu as the rest of us, so switching it up to suit your tastes is undoubtedly the best way to go.

Shochu is sometimes consumed as part of a cocktail of some sort. More often than not, *kōrui* (multiple-distilled) shochu is used as the alcoholic backbone of these drinks because it has very little remaining on the nose and palate after several tours through a patent still. Honkaku shochu can also be used, but it is probably best to use barley or rice varieties for mixing purposes as the flavors are more subtle than your average potato shochu. That said, mixing with soda or adding a cucumber stick could work with many types, and if you have time experiment with potato shochu and whatever mixers you have on hand. Alternatively, you can skip ahead to chapter nine for some popular shochu cocktail and liqueur mixing recipes.

A shochu server with a pair of shochu cups.

Another honkaku shochu serving style that can't be overlooked is *maewari*, the practice of preparing a full bottle of your own *mizuwari* mix at least 24 hours before you plan to drink it. This can be a good option if you have an upcoming dinner party and want to surprise your guests with a balanced and smooth drink that will pair nicely with a variety of dishes. You'll need to experiment on your own, but I usually make *maewari* with potato shochu and an 8:2 or 7:3 ratio. After capping the bottle, tip it back and forth to gently blend the ingredients and then store the bottle in a dark, cool place. Many good shochu bars have large clay shochu pots perched on the counter, and they are often used to dispense *maewari*. If the shochu bar or izakaya that you're visiting has some, definitely order it.

Drinking Vessels

Two beautiful cups made by Takuma Murakoshi.

The vessels that shochu is served in are just absolutely, positively gorgeous. Everything from colorful, hand-blown glass to artistically-glazed pottery is used to serve shochu. But ornamentation is not a prerequisite for determining what can or cannot hold your drink—there are few rules here. In fact, you probably already have some glassware that will work just fine. The stemless wine tumblers that are increasingly popular these days are perfect for capturing the bouquet of your shochu (not the best option for *oyuwari*, however). Smaller, stemmed glassware, such as brandy snifters, are also an excellent choice. Old-fashioned glasses will work wonders as well.

My collection of unique cups and tumblers has grown steadily over the years as my home inventory of shochu has blossomed. This is my favorite new shochu exploration hobby—collecting kilned vessels of all sizes, shapes, and colors. The artistry on display by Japan's potters is as exquisite as it is diverse, and many shops, including major department stores like Isetan and Mitsukoshi, carry a selection of beautiful pieces by both local artists and larger outfits such as Arita.

If you're after something a little more unique, then I would advise investing in some ceramic or kilned shochu cups. They range from the beautifully simple to the strikingly ornate, and they pair nicely with a small shochu kettle called a *kuro joka*. Depending on what they're made of, some can be placed over a small flame to warm the shochu inside. If you're planning to splurge on more traditional barware such as a *kuro joka* and drinking pottery, be sure to pick up a set of *sorakyū* as well. *Sorakyū* are small shochu cups that are shaped like rounded cones, and some varieties of *sorakyū* have a hole in the end. Yup, you read that correctly. As you're no doubt imagining, you have to block the hole with your finger while someone else pours, and there's no way to put the cup down without spilling its contents, so you know what that means—bottoms up!

A traditional *kuro joka* shochu kettle with two cups.

Time to taste

If you're drinking honkaku shochu, then you should be aware of the ways in which alcohol snobs/nerds the world over analyze their drink before any gulping comes into play. Honkaku shochu is a wonderfully-complex single distilled beverage, and that means, depending on the company you keep of course, you may find it acceptable or even necessary to subject your drink to any number of pre-imbibing rituals. Step one is to hold your glass up to observe the clarity of the drink. Even though a lot of people do it, don't hold your glass up to a source of light because the color of the drink will change. Instead, find a colorless backdrop, such as a white piece of paper or the sleeve of your boring work shirt. Now that the shochu industry is experimenting more with barrel aging, not all shochu are as colorless as water, and a pale hue can be a subtle hint about some of the aromas and flavors that you'll soon encounter. Of course, if your drink has been served in a vessel that is transparency-challenged, such as those made out of clay, then you can forego this part.

Many people will also swirl their drink around in the glass to help give the aromas a little boost. This is an excellent habit to get into as smell is the life and blood of taste. Just as you would with a glass of fine wine, go ahead and stick your nose down in there (without actually dunking it into your drink). Then think about it for a second. Does anything smell familiar? If so, then the sipping itself should be an entertaining experience because you'll be able to see if the aroma translates through to the tastes experienced on your palate. If not, then that's totally fine. The challenge then becomes simply determining whether or not the bouquet of aromas is pleasing for you. Is it strong or perhaps even a bit harsh on the nose? Or, conversely, are the aromas difficult to pick up? Good. Make a mental note. Or even better, pull out a pen and actually write something down. I routinely record tasting notes, both in text and audio, on my cell phone so that I can come back to them the next time that I try the same shochu. I actually do this for everything I drink that is expensive (i.e. most alcohol).

Now take a sip. One of the key things to think about is whether or not the drink feels balanced. By that I mean do the aromas match up in a measured way to what is actually happening when you move the shochu around your mouth. Swirl it around a bit. Aerate it by lightly pulling air in through your teeth. Make sure to dip your chin toward the table ever so slightly to avoid a fiery mist spraying into your lungs. Mixing the drink with oxygen will help you to taste it better, and you should let it move over your entire tongue for a few seconds before being sent down the hatch.

If you're the type, like me, who really enjoys this sort of thing, then go ahead and write your ideas down along with your comments on the ups and downs of the shochu's flavors.

Try to comment on how heavy or light the shochu felt while tasting it. Also, consider flavors such as sweet, sour, bitter, umami, and alcoholicity. Try to judge them against what you smelled when swirling the liquid around in your glass. Is everything in balance? If you can come to some kind of intelligible conclusion, then write it down. If not, start the process over again.

Learning to put words to tastes can take a lot of time and effort, so don't be discouraged if you aren't easily able to describe what you're sniffing and tasting. You'll be happy to hear that you can train your palate by simply drinking more shochu! I find that it's also helpful to get into the habit of smelling and tasting all sorts of food, everything from grains to toffee to venison, so that the brain is frequently reminded of all the flavors that are out there. The broader your experience with these aromas and flavors, the easier it will be to verbalize what your taste buds and brain are trying to decipher. (Chapter seven has a lot more to say about the lexicon of shochu, so there's help on the way if you've got a glass of shochu in your hand but can't think of what to say about it.) More importantly, it will become easier for you to differentiate between what you do and don't like.

Pay attention to the grains, spices, fruits, and alcohol vapors that present themselves. These characteristics will contribute heartily to the overall length and depth of the shochu. Length and depth are words that are frequently used when tasting other types of alcohol, especially wine. Both are incredibly subjective concepts that are nonetheless helpful in determining what you'd like to try a little bit more of. A shochu that is 'long' doesn't stop leaving an impression on your palate as it makes its way towards its final destination. Some shochu will present a big burst of flavor as soon as they enter the mouth and then die off shortly thereafter. In other words, the shochu stops 'short' during the middle of its journey. Personally, I enjoy shochu that maintain their richness from the front of the tongue to the back. For many shochu lovers, length is part and parcel with quality.

The depth of shochu is another vague concept that is worth tangling with. Depth is somewhat similar to complexity and seeks to acknowledge underlying threads of taste in the drink. Simplicity and straightforwardness are certainly welcome qualities in a shochu, but anything that tastes flat or lifeless should probably be mixed with tea to create an oolong cocktail.

As you slowly develop your shochu-admiring palate, one of the most exciting things is being able to assess what the wine folks call 'typicity.' This basically entails evaluating how closely the aromas and flavors that you experience adhere to the textbook characteristics of that shochu's type. For those that are turned off by the elitists from the wine crowd, there is reason to take heart. Many shochu are revered for their quirkiness and willful flaunting of the characteristics that would normally cause people to assess them as being true to type. One can easily find *mugi* shochu that tastes like light rum and then others that are more like low-cal whiskey. These are quirks to delight in, not disparage. If you happen to be in Japan, find a good shochu bar or restaurant and ask for something similar to what you enjoy. After that, if you're feeling adventurous, ask to try something rare or out of the ordinary for its type.

Chapter 7
Shochu pairing and sharing

This chapter begins with an introduction to the vocabulary that can be used to describe the smells and flavors you experience while enjoying your next glass of shochu. The bank of words below is by no means exclusive to shochu, and you may find that your hard-earned beer or whiskey vocabulary can be repurposed here. The key is to be as flexible as possible, and use whatever language comes to mind when trying to ascribe words to what your senses pick up.

Later in the chapter there is a guide to sharing your shochu obsession with others. You'll find a breakdown of each major ingredient type into flavor and aroma groups as well as general hints about how to pair them with food. Thankfully, shochu is incredibly versatile, ranking right up there with beer and wine in terms of its ability to complement and enhance the flavors in the dishes that it is paired with. Whether you're enjoying meat, fish, vegetarian, or dessert, there are myriad bottles to suit your fancy. Much of the art of pairing will come down to personal taste, but there are some simple guidelines for pairing food with alcohol that are more or less consistent around the world. I have taken the liberty of including several of my favorite pairing options at the end of each ingredient section.

Smell and taste
Because it can take a while to hone one's tasting lexicon, I thought I'd include a list of common words that are used to interpret the many messages that our taste buds send to our brains any time we smell and taste something. This list is not exhaustive, but hopefully it will give you a head start when it comes to matching words to tastes.

- Potato: baked potato; sweet potato; steamed potato

- Barley: barley flour; wafer; bread; rye bread

- Rice: rice *kōji*; saké lees; rice cake; wild rice

- Other grains: oats; oatmeal; corn flakes; wheat bread; straw

- Sugar: molasses; rum; brown sugar; maple syrup; sugared candy; honey

- Dairy: milk; fresh cream; butter; yogurt; custard; cheese

- Vegetables: cucumber; soy; radish; carrot; celery; tomato; eggplant; onion

- Fruit: peach; orange; lychee; melon; pear; apricot; lemon; lime; banana; apple; cherry; grapefruit; sudachi; raspberry; strawberry; blueberry

- Nuts: sesame; cashew; peanut; almond; walnut; chestnut

- Tea: oolong; green; apple; jasmine; brown rice; barley

- Spice: cinnamon; vanilla; black pepper; cumin; nutmeg; clove; anise; perilla

- Flowers: lotus; lily; rose; lavender; cyclamen; acacia; lilac

- Mint: sage; coriander; thyme; parsley; peppermint; spearmint

- Trees: oak; cypress; cedar; pine; magnolia

And there are so many more! Taste is such a subjective experience, so you should liberally add to this list. For instance, I didn't include anything about mushrooms here, but I've sensed porcini in my shochu before. And I didn't mention dried fruit either, but I'm sure you'll run into a shochu that reminds you of raisins before too long. One barley shochu in my home bar has an aroma that reminds me of freshly woven tatami mats. Some shochu have a roasted quality to them or maybe even something more like smokiness. You are limited only by your experience and memory, and don't be shy if what you're drinking has a mineral, metallic, or plastic side to it. I remember once hearing the wine guy, Gary Vaynerchuk, remark that a wine he was tasting reminded him of licking a racquetball. It certainly wasn't a compliment, but I admire his ability to associate taste with aspects of everyday life that aren't normally brought into this type of conversation.

Don't lose heart if you find it difficult to separate flavors and describe them individually. Start with a description of the general first, and then work from there. In other words, it may be advantageous to look for the big family names of taste like sweet, sour, salty, bitter, and umami. Sorry to disappoint you, but I'm not going to put one of those diagrams of the human tongue on this page and draw arrows to the segregated groups of taste buds that we've been taught for more than a hundred years to think are exclusive, walled-off zones. What a load of bull. Science has long since found that most of the tongue can sense all of these flavors, and you should be very careful not to limit your understanding of taste to the pseudo-science of more than a century ago. Just because sweetness is registering on the side of your tongue—historically the sacred neighborhood where sour is sensed—doesn't mean that it's not sweet! All right, rant finished.

You can help your nose and tongue out by doing a little bit of extra practice. What follows is textbook palate development, and it's quite simple. Pick one of the flavor categories above and grab a bunch of wine glasses. Find some examples from the category that you chose and place them inside the glasses. For example, if you choose 'fruit' as your category, then chop up some banana, table grapes, orange, kiwi, or any other fruit that you have easy access to, and place them in separate glasses. Now, just as if you were inhaling the bouquet from a glass of shochu, stick your nose in there and really think about the smell. Naturally, do the same with the other glasses that you've prepared, and if you want to take it a step further, put some shochu in a wine glass as well and see if you can find any aromas that match. Maybe none of them will, but that's totally fine. At least you know for sure what the drink does *not* remind you of, and that information is helpful, too.

Spreading the Love

As shochu's popularity continues to grow both domestically and abroad, there is an increasing number of folks who ask the question, "Hey, what is this stuff?" Fellow shochu savant, Stephen Lyman, spends a lot of his time organizing tastings and demystifying shochu for the residents of New York City.

He remarked that there is a steadily growing awareness of shochu in the United States but that the places serving it often choose the wrong metaphors when describing it. Lyman asserts that "the one thing that I think we need to avoid is calling it 'Japanese vodka.' It's a terrible way to introduce *jōatsu* versions, *imo*, and awamori."

Indeed, while conducting the research for this book, I was in contact with restaurant industry professionals from all over the globe, many of whom have recently begun carrying shochu in addition to the nihonshu that was already on their menus. During these discussions, I found that many people had a hard time educating their customers about what shochu is and is not. If you happen to work in a place that deals with shochu, or even if you just want to explain this wonderful world to your curious friends, you may experience similar difficulties. Due to the diversity of the drinks that are called shochu, finding a starting point for your explanation and suggesting a selection from the menu can feel like a crap-shoot. Chapter two has some helpful information about what shochu is *not*, and this chapter is designed to help aficionados explain what it *is*.

Over the near to medium term, the number of people around the world with zero knowledge of shochu will remain high. I routinely run into people living in Japan who still have almost no idea how shochu is different from nihonshu, what ingredients are used to make it, how much alcohol is in it, and what it tastes like. If you are talking to someone who is a complete shochu beginner, then one strategy is to talk about aroma and taste on a sliding scale from simple to complex. To assist with explaining the strength of the different flavors in play, I created a chart based on a Cartesian plane developed by the Sake Service Institute (SSI). The chart plots shochu according to what is happening on the nose and in the mouth, so to speak.

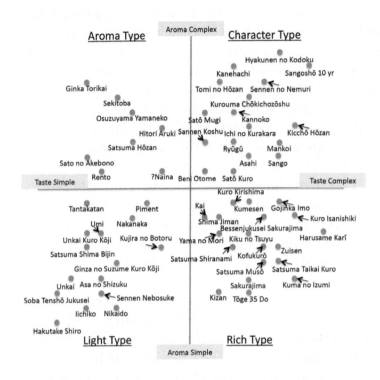

The vertical y-axis ranks the complexity of the aromas that are present, and the x-axis ranks depth of taste with more complex shochu sliding to the right. The quadrants of this chart are labeled (clockwise from upper left) Aroma Type, Character Type, Rich Type, and Light Type.

If you have a whiskey drinker on your hands, then you can probably begin with something that is on the right side of the y-axis since they may have an easier time appreciating the layers of taste and earthy notes in the drink. For example, a *Kannoko* barley shochu or *Satō Kuro Potato (imo) shochu* on the rocks might be a good way to start. If you're worried about overwhelming your customer or drinking partner right from the start, suggest a *mizuwari* mix, or pick a bottle from the left side of the vertical line. *Satsuma Shima Bijin*, a potato shochu made with white *kōji*, has a much lighter flavor profile, and one of the more famous brown sugar shochu, *Rento*, is pleasantly sweet. Perhaps the safest starting point is to choose something from the Light Type quadrant. *Shiro*, a well-marketed rice shochu produced by Hakutake Distillery, and *Nakanaka* barley shochu by Kuroki Honten in Miyazaki Prefecture, are two such choices from this portion of the chart, and both are very approachable even for shochu novices.

Long term, however, there will be a lot more people out there who know a little about shochu and want to learn more. I tend to start by talking about potatoes, rice, or another favorite base veggie with more experienced customers. Maybe they've tried potato shochu before, but they'd like to try one made with a different type of *kōji*. Or perhaps they know and like barley shochu but want to try something that has been barrel-aged to see how that affects the taste. I've had lots of people tell me that they wanted to try something that was a little 'different' or that they can't buy easily where they're from. In this case, you may find it helpful to begin with the ingredients that are used in shochu production and then blend in aspects of the aroma and flavor chart as necessary.

Potato (*imo*) shochu

In terms of *imo*, there are myriad specimens from all four of the quadrants. For a light, refreshing, and clean potato shochu, *Umi* might hit the spot, as would any other potato contestant from the Light Type quadrant. *Umi* happens to be an excellent starter potato shochu for the uninitiated, and it is often recommended to tourists here in Japan when they say that they would like to try one. Light Type bottles can also be a good bet for the first drink of the night or for when you want something light to go with an appetizer. I think this kind of potato shochu also pairs nicely with entrees that are dominated by vegetables, and while I prefer to enjoy them straight, they're delightful both *mizuwari* and on the rocks.

For something with a more pronounced sweetness, a bit showier, move up to the Aroma Type zone and reach for a bottle of *Satsuma Hōzan* or *Hitori Aruki*. You'll find more orange and sweet potato notes in these drinks, even though they may not be very robust flavor-wise. I would recommend serving these on the rocks so that the delicate bouquet doesn't get bludgeoned by whatever you choose to put in the glass. There are a lot of shochu made with yellow *kōji* in this group, and several use *joy white* potatoes.

Koganesengan potatoes and white *kōji* are often used in so-called Rich Type shochu, and this is the group that tends to pair extremely well with the chicken and pork dishes of Kyushu Island. The very well-known and loved, *Satsuma Shiranami*, and another Kagoshima classic, *Sakurajima*, are two excellent examples of shochu that have a richer and more complex taste than anything else mentioned so far in this section. They are often very nice in an *oyuwari* mix because the hot water helps to round out the aromas and temper any bitterness that would be encountered when drinking them straight. These drinks work well as an accompaniment to bonito and other flavorful fish.

The fourth group of shochu contestants in the potato family straddle the x-axis between the Rich Type and Character Type quadrants, and they're a good option for folks who want a heartier and fuller drink. Many of these shochu use black *kōji* which can add both sweet and earthy accents while teasing out and highlighting the potato's natural flavors. *Kuro Kirishima*, *Satsuma Taikai Kuro*, *Kicchō Hōzan*, and *Ishinokurakara* are all heavier hitters in terms of aroma and flavor profile, and they are very nice both on the rocks and as the larger portion of an *oyuwari* mix.

The drinks in that final group can stand up to spicy foods and team well with meat, fried food, and many Chinese dishes. As a general rule, the prickly sweet of many *imo* shochu plays nicely with earthy-tasting fish. Bonito was mentioned earlier, and I would also include mackerel and oysters here amongst many others. You'll also find that *oden* goes well with shochu from the left side of the grid where the flavors are relatively tamer. Chicken and pork are always going to be safe bets here as well, which is not much of a surprise. Both are staples of Kyushu cuisine, and I'm a big fan of pairing *imo* with pork chops, bacon, and sausage.

Barley (*mugi*) shochu
This family of subtle and delicious shochu runs neck-and-neck with *imo* in terms of liters shipped and consumed in Japan. And when you're looking for a light and refreshing drink, or perhaps you're having drinks with someone who is new to shochu, I recommend starting here in the Light Type zone

with a glass of *Nikaido* or *Iichiko*. It was *Iichiko*, in fact, that really helped fuel the first modern shochu boom when it was introduced in 1979 by Sanwa Shurui. Its smooth finish has helped it earn the rank of best-seller in Japan, and for the past several years Sanwa Shurui has raked in more than 50 billion yen annually from sales of the various *Iichiko* permutations in its lineup (roughly 20 billion yen more than its nearest competitor, Kirishima Shuzō). You can serve *Nikaido* and *Iichiko* any way you like—they won't let you down.

We're going to cross the grid diagonally into the Character Type quadrant for the next group of *mugi* shochu. They are characterized by being quite flavorful and fragrant, especially when compared with *Iichiko* or many of the others classified as Light Type. These shochu pair well with aromatic grilled dishes, and are best served on the rocks or straight. *Kanehachi* is an excellent selection from this group. Along with the expected barley notes, it carries a bit of cacao. *Satō Mugi* is another nice bottle from this group if you can find it.

Another group of *mugi* is bunched up in the corner of the same quadrant, but these guys are generally barrel-aged. The casks give them their golden coloring, and they are hugely popular for their complex yet smooth flavor profiles. Introduced in 1985, Kuroki Honten's *Hyakunen no Kodoku* sets the standard, and it has the price point to match. I adore the hints of almond and vanilla in this shochu, and I think that single malt drinkers might find something to love here. Another important member of this group is *Kannoko* which is available in many cities around the globe these days. These two beautiful *mugi* should really be enjoyed neat, but rocks are fine if that's your thing. I might also recommend a drop or two of mineral water if you're trying to find a middle ground between the two serving styles. *Hyakunen no Kodoku*, *Kannoko*, and others like them are fantastic as after-dinner libations.

A chicken dish in a Miyazaki Prefecture izakaya.

The last grouping is from down in the Rich Type quadrant, and it features hearty labels such as *Yama no Mori* which is a marvelous contribution from the great Iki shochu tradition of Nagasaki Prefecture. *Yama no Mori* employs a rice starter mash and it is generally recommended that you use an *oyuwari* mix for these in either a 6:4 or 5:5 ratio. I also like *Kofukurō* which presents a robust roasted quality. The Rich Type barley shochu go equally well with pickled vegetables and fried foods, but the same can be said for most *mugi*. They also pair nicely with sushi rolls (*norimaki*), whether it's something simple like cucumber or tuna wrapped inside or a more complex version like *makizushi*. Additionally, you can't go wrong with a nice, fat steak while sipping a glass of barley shochu on the rocks. And we shouldn't forget that chicken dishes are very common in Miyazaki and Nagasaki Prefectures, parts of Kyushu that are famous for their *mugi* labels. If I had to choose, I'd say that chicken thigh is the best option for pairing with barley shochu since the meat is darker and tends to be more flavorful.

Rice (*kome*) shochu

Contrary to what you might expect given the neutrality of the base ingredient, there are some complex rice shochu out there that will pair beautifully with a plethora of dishes, from fish to pasta to marinated veggies. If we start in the Light Type corner, then you're not going to be able to avoid *Hakutake Shiro*. Produced by Takahashi Shuzō in Kumamoto Prefecture and shipped to many major markets outside of Japan, this *kome* shochu gets its soft and clean taste from low pressure (*gen'atsu*) distillation and aging in a stainless steel tank. Many have argued that this is an excellent starting point for times when enjoying dinner with a shochu novice.

For something with a bit more excitement, especially in the bouquet, you can't help but recommend *Ginka Torikai* from the Aroma Type zone, a rice shochu that has undeniable *ginjō* nihonshu qualities. The distiller uses yellow *kōji kin* spores with the steamed rice, the same type used in the lion's share of nihonshu production, so you might smell something a bit more tropical or fruity with this one. Tank aged for six months, I love *Ginka Torikai* on the rocks or mixed with a touch of cold water, and it's a great aperitif.

Last but not least, let's take a peak at the Rich Type quadrant where we can find *kome* with a bit more earthy oomph. Unlike the two bottles already mentioned in this section, these guys tend to be distilled at atmospheric pressure (*jōatsu*), a higher temperature boil that will allow more of the esters from the other ingredients in the mash to escape from the still. *Kuma no Izumi*, also from Kumamoto Prefecture, is a bit more traditional in that it uses white rather than yellow *kōji kin* spores, lending the bottled product a relatively complex finish. Aged for at least two years in a steel tank, you'll enjoy this with either hot or cool water mixed in, or with ice.

Rice shochu works just fine with sushi, but I think it's even better with sashimi. Oysters and caviar will both find balance alongside a glass of *kome* shochu on the rocks. I've also found that pasta with meat sauce and many types of cheese can be complemented by rice shochu. Try it alongside chicken dishes (breast), oily or smoked dishes, and even pickled vegetables. Thanks to its light palate and softly sweet notes, rice shochu can accompany a wide variety of appetizers and entrees.

Awamori
Unlike rice shochu, awamori is rarely accused of being subtle. We're mostly dealing with two quadrants here, Rich and Character, and there are several good choices for whichever way you want to go. Remember that black *kōji kin* is required in the production of awamori, and most awamori is bottled at 30% ABV or above, so we're dealing with far more robust flavors and aromas.

In the Rich Type zone, there's a wide range of awamori that stretches from the mildly earthy to the brash and heavy. If you're looking for an awamori on the milder side, then reach for something with a lower ABV (20-25%) or which is an atmospheric/low pressure distillation blend. However, most of what's available commercially is rammed with complexity and less muted on the nose. *Harusame Karī* is a nice option from the southern part of Okinawa's main island, not far from Naha. It's a balanced awamori with a hint of sweetness and a clean finish, and I like this one because it's just as good with warm water as it is on the rocks.

Up in the Character Type quadrant, you've got a number of aged awamori that exhibit beautiful spicy notes and hints of vanilla on the nose. 10-year-old *Sangoshō* is a delicious example of how awamori can mature with age. You may catch a nutty sweetness in this 86 proof tipple if you don't drown it in water or dunk too many ice cubes in it. I like to drink *Sangoshō* 10-year neat after a meal because it's a round and complex offering from the good people at Yamakawa Shuzō.

If it grows together, it goes together, so Okinawan cuisine (*gōya chanpurū*!) will naturally pair very nicely with awamori, and one of the best places to try awamori when traveling in Japan is to visit an Okinawan restaurant (especially if you can get to Okinawa itself!). Tokyo and Osaka have several good ones, and they'll likely have no fewer than 10 awamori in stock. Thanks to various pairing experiments conducted at home, I've found that awamori goes well with everything from spare ribs to lasagna, and you might want to order a glass the next time you're having tuna sashimi. I'm also partial to awamori with my *shabu shabu*, and all sorts of pork, beef, and chicken (thigh) dishes can be enjoyed alongside shochu's beloved relative to the south.

A *gōya* appetizer to go with your glass of awamori.

Brown sugar (*kokutō*) shochu

Shochu novices would do well to start in the Aroma Type quadrant where they'll find the likes of *Rento* and *Sato no Akebono*. *Kokutō* like these often have a rum reminder on the nose with easily recognizable sugar cane notes that are wonderful straight, on the rocks, or with cold water. Thanks to their being distilled at reduced pressure, they are very smooth going down and are sometimes used in cocktails as a low-cal rum substitute.

The other large group of *kokutō* shochu are clustered in the Character Type quadrant, and more often than not they are distilled at atmospheric pressure. They have more depth and a rounded caramel sweetness that's to die for. I'm talking about brown sugar shochu like *Mankoi* and *Ryūgū* (both 30% ABV). I love the mineral and spice notes in some of the bottles that can be found in this range, and they can hold their own against a variety of savory or bitter dishes. I also recommend these shochu when grilling. Like their counterparts from the Aroma Type zone, they play well on the rocks or *mizuwari*. You might even like them *oyuwari*, so give that a whirl any time the weather calls for it.

The fragrant yet light *kokutō* shochu from the Aroma Type zone obviously go well with sweet dishes. Accordingly, don't miss the opportunity to try these alongside a lobster or crab dinner as they have an uncanny ability to accentuate the natural sweetness of seafood. The drink's sweetness is also a nice accompaniment to cheese fondue or pasta with a cream-based sauce. If you are serving tomato and mozzarella slices as an appetizer at your next dinner party, then make sure you have some chilled brown sugar shochu ready as an aperitif. I would also recommend a *kokutō* any time you are lucky enough to be enjoying *sukiyaki* with friends.

Buckwheat (*soba*) shochu
Many *soba* shochu are safely ensconced in the Light Type corner of the chart. The only *soba* contestant in chapter eight, *Unkai*, is not only the standard-bearer of its type, but is also incredibly easy to drink. I highly recommend *soba* shochu as a beginner's first tipple. Other recommendations from this quadrant would be *Soba Tenshō Jukusei*, which is excellent consumed straight or on the rocks, and *Unkai's* younger sibling, *Unkai Kuro Kōji*. These drinks are famous for pairing with soba noodles, and particularly the warm *soba*-flavored soup left after the noodles are gone. I would also argue that *soba* shochu pairs very well with one of my favorite izakaya staples, *butaniku no shōgayaki*.

Soba shochu is not known for having a powerful bouquet, but it is possible to find bottles that give you more to think about on the palate. Crossing the y-axis of the chart we can find some more flavorful shochu in the Rich Type zone.

Nagano Prefecture, a popular weekend getaway destination for Tokyoites, is actually home to a few *soba* shochu distilleries. Debuting in 1975, *Tōge* was a step in a new direction for Kitsukura Shuzō, a distillery that had made *kasutori* shochu for many years. I recommend *Tōge 35 Do* as a relatively complex buckwheat option. Chikuma Nishiki Shuzō's *Kizan* is another beauty from Nagano that is aged in oak barrels. These richer, 35% ABV shochu go particularly well with fried oysters.

Chapter 8
Recommended shochu

This is a short list of shochu that I like. Every single one of these bottles (all 33 of them) is from my personal collection, and please take my word for it that I have tested each for quality. The reviews, I trust it goes without saying, are completely independent. I hope that you will be able to find at least a few of these at a liquor shop, restaurant, or internet retailer near you. Please bear in mind that my underlined serving style recommendations might not be for everyone, so if you're not enthused, don't worry. Keep adjusting until you find a style that suits your personal taste.

I have done my utmost to track down the specifics of each bottle's *kōji kin* and distillation method, but I was not 100% successful. We'll just chalk this up to "trade secrets" since both are inseparable from the quality of the final product. Check the comments for each bottle to find extra notes on the ingredients and any aging-related information that I was able to uncover. However, please bear in mind that the details listed below are not the entire picture. Just because a distillery tells people that a specific shochu was distilled at atmospheric pressure does not mean that it hasn't been blended with a previous year's shochu to help tame some of its more bracing fragrances and flavors. There's a lot of unannounced blending that goes on, and it's not something that distilleries are currently obliged to acknowledge on the label, although many do. The takeaway? There's a whole lot more to the story of each shochu listed here than meets the eye.

Potato (*imo*) shochu

Bessenjukusei Sakurajima (別撰熟成 桜島 / べっせんじゅくせい　さくらじま) Hombo Shuzō, Kagoshima Prefecture, Japan
ABV: 25%, *Kōji*: rice (black *kōji kin*)
Distillation: atmospheric distillation
Recommended serving style:
    Neat   **Rocks**
    Mizuwari   ***Oyuwari***

Comments: This is Hombo Distillery's famous Sakurajima *genshu* that has been aged. It's made from 100% Kagoshima Prefecture *koganesengan* sweet potatoes, and the aging rounds the sweet and spicy notes of its younger relative. The spice is still there on the nose though, and if you try it neat you'll notice that it's a medium-bodied spirit with wisps of apple and pear. Of the three serving options that are highlighted above, my opinion is that *mizuwari* or ice are the two best ways to go.

Gojinka Imo (御神火 芋 / ごじんか い も) Taniguchi Shuzō, Tokyo, Japan
ABV: 25-26%, *Kōji*: barley (white *kōji kin*)
Distillation: atmospheric pressure
Recommended serving style:
Neat   **Rocks**
Mizuwari   ***Oyuwari***

Comments: Gojinka Imo is a unique potato shochu. It's headlined by *beni azuma* potatoes rather than the more common *koganesengan*, and the *kōji* is made with barley. This intriguing blend of potato and barley flavors is tank aged for one year before bottling at Taniguchi Shuzō on Oshima Island, which is technically part of Tokyo. The result is one of butter on the nose and a candy sweetness reminiscent of caramel everywhere else. Try it on the rocks or neat if you're pairing it with food that has some punch. However, in terms of serving styles, I highly recommend trying this shochu *oyuwari*. The bouquet is gorgeously layered when hot water is added, and it can stand up to side dishes that have strong aromas. Notice the barley coming through on the finish.

Kai (界 / かい) Higashi Shuzō, Kagoshima Prefecture, Japan
ABV: 25%, *Kōji*: rice (black and white *kōji kin*)
Distillation: unknown
Recommended serving style:
     Neat   **<u>Rocks</u>**
     Mizuwari   ***<u>Oyuwari</u>***

Comments: This is a fruity, soft, and round *imo* shochu that is made using both black and white *kōji kin*. Aged for more than two years, the aromas are sweet and subdued potato (*koganesengan*). Kai's elegance continues through the attack and into the mid-palate where bright hints of green melon seem to drop the liquid's temperature if you try it neat. This is the kind of *imo* that can lure newcomers into shochu's grip.

Kujira no Botoru (くじら の ボトル)
Taikai Shuzō, Kagoshima Prefecture,
Japan
ABV: 25%, *Kōji*: rice (white *kōji kin*)
Distillation: atmospheric pressure
Recommended serving style:
    Neat   Rocks
    Mizuwari   ***Oyuwari***

Comments: The good folks at Taikai Distillery recommend serving Kujira *oyuwari* at between 40-50 degrees Celsius. This is a standard bottle in my home bar, and it always makes me chuckle that they chose to write "Kugilla" in English. That bucks a couple of the rules governing how to represent Japanese words, in this case 'whale,' in English, but who am I to complain? Kujira has an understated attack and its medium-bodied softness makes it very easy to drink. Try it *nurukan* to feel the flavors come to life.

Kuro Isanishiki (黒 伊佐錦 / くろ い さにしき) Ohkuchi Shuzō, Kagoshima Prefecture, Japan
ABV: 25%, *Kōji*: rice (black *kōji kin*)
Distillation: atmospheric distillation
Recommended serving style:
Neat   **Rocks**
Mizuwari   *Oyuwari*

Comments: Tank aged and slightly floral nose with full flavor. This is Isanishiki made with black *kōji* and, of course, *koganesengan* sweet potatoes. It has a nice balance of light sweet and spicy notes with a straightforward attack when it hits the palate. This is a versatile drink that can be enjoyed many different ways, but if you visit Kagoshima City at the heart of *imo* shochu country, you'll quickly find that Kuro Isanishiki lines the back walls of many restaurants and izakaya, and it's routinely consumed *oyuwari*. I highly recommend that you do the same.

Kuro Kirishima (黒霧島 / くろ きりしま)
Kirishima Shuzō, Miyazaki Prefecture, Japan
ABV: 25%, *Kōji*: rice (black *kōji kin*)
Distillation: atmospheric distillation
Recommended serving style:

Neat	**Rocks**
Mizuwari	*Oyuwari*

Comments: This *imo* shochu has already traveled far and wide—folks with access to izakaya or decent Japanese restaurants worldwide will likely have seen this bottle on a restaurant menu somewhere. Tank aged, Kuro Kirishima has a clean, dry finish. It's one of those rare *imo* shochu that might actually be better on the rocks than *oyuwari*. *Koganesengan* sweet potatoes and black *kōji* are used here to create a full-bodied, round sweetness that is a solid choice before or during a meal.

?Naina (？ないな) Meigetsu Shuzō, Miyazaki Prefecture, Japan
ABV: 25%, *Kōji*: *japonica* and *indica* rice (white *kōji kin*)
Distillation: atmospheric pressure
Recommended serving style:

| Neat | **<u>Rocks</u>** |
| *Mizuwari* | ***<u>Oyuwari</u>*** |

Comments: I don't know why they put the question mark before the name of the shochu, but I just wanted to assure you that it isn't a typo. Apparently *"Naina"* is an expression used in Miyazaki Prefecture that can loosely be translated to, "Why?" or "Huh?" I suppose the name is appropriate because this bottle is an *imo* shochu (*koganesengan*) blended with a little bit of rice shochu. It's a creative approach that works well. The nose is reminiscent of steamed *beni azuma* potatoes, and it's light-bodied with a short finish. I daresay that there's a breadiness to it, especially when you take that first breath after it goes down the hatch.

Osuzuyama Yamaneko (尾鈴山 山ね
こ / おすずやま やまねこ) Osuzuyama
Jōryūjo, Miyazaki Prefecture, Japan
ABV: 25%, *Kōji*: rice (white *kōji kin*)
Distillation: atmospheric pressure
Recommended serving style:

| Neat | **<u>Rocks</u>** |
| *Mizuwari* | *<u>Oyuwari</u>* |

Comments: Note that this drink is generally known by its
nickname, Yamaneko, rather than the full title listed above.
Osuzuyama Jōryūjo, the distillery that is responsible for the
wonderful Yamaneko (or 'mountain cat' in Japanese), is the
type of place that James Bond would own if he ever made
shochu. It's hidden up on Osuzu Mountain, and it has a cozy
hideout quality thanks to its seclusion. It's owned by the
Kuroki family whom, as you may have noticed from reading
through this book, I have a huge amount of respect for due to
the way that they try to source and recycle everything locally.
In other words, Kuroki Honten and Osuzuyama Jōryūjo
are run by the same people, but the latter is a younger part
of their business, and as such it has a bit more liberty to try
new things and rewrite the playbook, so to speak. *Joy white*
sweet potatoes (aka Kyushu #108) are used here rather than
the standard *koganesengan*, and the *tōji* uses a proprietary

yeast that was developed in-house. Tank-aged for more than two years, Yamaneko is fragrant, fruity with a sharp finish, and perfect pretty much any way you serve it. This shochu works very well either before or during a meal, and I like how it pairs with sashimi (especially tuna), pork, and chicken *tataki* (chicken that has been lightly seared over a charcoal flame).

Satsuma Musō - Aka Raberu (さつま無双 - 赤 ラベル / さつま むそう - あか らべる) Satsuma Musō, Kagoshima Prefecture, Japan
ABV: 25%, *Kōji*: rice (white *kōji kin*)
Distillation: atmospheric pressure
Recommended serving style:

Neat	**Rocks**
Mizuwari	*Oyuwari*

Comments: "Aka Raberu" means red label in Japanese, and it's an indication that Satsuma Musō, a distillery that is supported in part by the Kagoshima Prefectural Government, produces a line of shochu bearing differently colored outfits. I'm quite partial to their black label *imo* that also features *koganesengan* but opts for black *kōji* and finds a nice balance between sweet and rich. The red label, on the other hand, is a bit more subtle and smoother both on the attack and finish. There's something in the bouquet that reminds me of Japanese cypress trees, plus the expected sweet fruit scents. I usually drink this on the rocks because it feels fuller that way, but it's also quite nice *oyuwari* where the sweet notes (banana) stand out.

Satsuma Shima Bijin (さつま 島 美人 / さつま しま びじん) Nagashima Kenjō, Kagoshima Prefecture, Japan
ABV: 25%, *Kōji*: rice (white *kōji kin*)
Distillation: atmospheric pressure
Recommended serving style:
Neat   Rocks
Mizuwari   ***Oyuwari***

Comments: Made with dependable *koganesengan* sweet potatoes, this is a very light and simple *imo* shochu that, to borrow a beer drinking term, is quite 'sessionable.' It's subdued to the point that it's not uncommon to see folks drinking it neat at the bar, but it's good *oyuwari* because the warmth will draw out a slight earthiness, almost like standing next to a veggie garden in the morning. There's not a whole lot of potato on the nose or at the finish when it goes down the hatch, so it can be considered a good starter for people who want to try *imo* shochu but aren't yet used to the drink's signature earthy sweetness.

Satsuma Shiranami (さつま 白波 / さつ
ま しらなみ) Satsuma Shuzō, Kagoshima
Prefecture, Japan
ABV: 25%, *Kōji*: rice (white *kōji kin*)
Distillation: atmospheric pressure
Recommended serving style:

Neat	**Rocks**
Mizuwari	***Oyuwari***

Comments: Even if you've never been to Japan before, you
may have seen this iconic label on the menu of an izakaya or
Japanese restaurant. Shiranami used to be the local drink in
Kagoshima City before it started to reach into new markets,
including some outside of Japan, and saw its place at home
taken by Kuro Isanishiki (earlier in this section). Made with
koganesengan sweet potatoes, this *imo* shochu balances sweet
and savory. Try it *oyuwari* or *nurukan* for a good look at the
sweet and dry notes, or serve on the rocks with sushi or chicken
teriyaki.

Sekitoba (赤兎馬 / せきとば) Hamada
Shuzō, Kagoshima Prefecture, Japan
ABV: 25%, *Kōji*: rice (white *kōji kin*)
Distillation: atmospheric pressure
Recommended serving style:

Neat   **Rocks**
Mizuwari   *Oyuwari*

Comments: This *koganesengan* sweet potato shochu presents a candy-like sweetness on the nose. The attack is light and it displays a medium-bodied smoothness with rounded and almost sugared potato notes. It awakens the roof of the palate with a refreshing yet relatively short impression. This is a bottle that I always have at least one of in the cupboard, and I generally drink it neat. It's a bit lighter than some of the other *imo* bottles in this list, so it has found favor with both veteran and novice shochu disciples alike.

Tomi no Hōzan (富 乃 宝山 / とみ の ほうざん) Nishi Shuzō, Kagoshima Prefecture, Japan
ABV: 25%, *Kōji*: rice (yellow *kōji kin*)
Distillation: low and atmospheric pressure blend
Recommended serving style:
<u>**Neat**</u>   <u>**Rocks**</u>
<u>*Mizuwari*</u>   *Oyuwari*

Comments: This is a delightful drink made with the same *kōji* (yellow) used in nihonshu production. With *koganesengan* sweet potatoes added to the second stage of fermentation, and featuring a careful blend of *gen'atsu* and *jōatsu* distillates, the result is a complex yet highly drinkable shochu that is best on the rocks. It will remind you of *ginjō* grade nihonshu with its floral bouquet that at times imitates Muscat grapes, and it pairs well with spare ribs, potato chips, or white fish. I wish that they would put out a *genshu* version of this, aged for a couple of years, so that I could sip it straight after dinner.

 **Umi** (海 / うみ) Taikai Shuzō, Kagoshima Prefecture, Japan
ABV: 25%, *Kōji*: rice (yellow *kōji kin*)
Distillation: low pressure
Recommended serving style:
    Neat   **Rocks**
    Mizuwari   *Oyuwari*

Comments: This is the perfect shochu for someone who wants to get into *imo*, but finds strong potato aromas to be off-putting. Umi has very subtle potato sweetness on the nose, but it's actually a bit more floral than anything else. The combination of low pressure distillation and yellow *kōji* leads to a shochu that is sweet and very easy to drink. You can serve this over crushed ice, or mix it *maewari* a day before you plan to drink it. Chill it and then serve it in a wine glass to catch the whisper of rose petals in the bouquet.

Barley (*mugi*) shochu

Mugi is what I drink when I go to baseball games in Tokyo. I'm a huge fan of the aptly named Tokyo Swallows, an enormously underrated team, and I like to bring a thermos of *mugi* shochu with me to the games. I know what you're thinking: you can bring alcohol with you to a game?! The answer is yes (and no). At Jingu Stadium, the home of the Swallows, they check your bag for cans and bottles of hooch, but they never bat an eyelash at the 1.2 liter thermos hanging by a nylon strap between my shoulder blades. Happy times always ensue.

Ginza no Suzume Kuro *Kōji* (銀座 の すずめ 黒 麹 / ぎんざ の すずめ くろ こ うじ) Yatsushika Shuzō, Ōita Prefecture, Japan
ABV: 25%, *Kōji*: barley (black *kōji kin*)
Distillation: low and atmospheric pressure blend
Recommended serving style:
　　　Neat　　　　**Rocks**
　　　Mizuwari　　*Oyuwari*

Comments: This *mugi* shochu is actually a blend of four different distillates, some of it using a vacuum pressure pot still, and the rest coming from a more conventional atmospheric pressure still. The result is a flavorful, easy-drinking, modern interpretation of shochu built on 100% barley *kōji* (no rice used in the mash). Fans love it for its depth and smoothness.

Kurouma Chōkichozōshu (くろうま 長期貯蔵酒 / くろうま ちょうきちょぞうしゅう) Kagura Shuzō, Miyazaki Prefecture, Japan
ABV: 25%, *Kōji*: barley (white *kōji kin*)
Distillation: low pressure
Recommended serving style:

| **Neat** | **Rocks** |
| *Mizuwari* | *Oyuwari* |

Comments: This barrel-aged *mugi* shochu smells and tastes like a mild whiskey. Made from 100% domestic two-row barley, it works well on the rocks, but you could also add cola to it for a bit of cocktail action. Low alkaline water and three-plus years of aging lead to a rounded and polite sweetness that is perfect after a light meal.

Sennen no Nemuri (千年 の 眠り / せん ねん の ねむり) Shinozaki Co., Fukuoka Prefecture, Japan
ABV: 40%, *Kōji*: barley (*kōji kin* type unknown)
Distillation: atmospheric pressure
Recommended serving style:

<u>**Neat**</u>	<u>**Rocks**</u>
<u>***Mizuwari***</u>	<u>***Oyuwari***</u>

Comments: Cask-aged for between three and eight years, whiskey drinkers will enjoy this. It has a light straw hue and carries a cherry-sweet attack which matches the nose and gives way to a full-bodied vanilla, barley, and red citrus palate. The finish is clean, even surprisingly so, given the complexity of this *mugi* shochu. This is a great after-dinner treat, either on the rocks or solo in a brandy snifter.

Shima Jiman (嶋 自慢 / しま じまん)
Miyahara Shuzō, Tokyo, Japan
ABV: 25%, *Kōji*: barley (white *kōji kin*)
Distillation: atmospheric pressure
Recommended serving style:
    Neat   **Rocks**
    Mizuwari   *Oyuwari*

Comments: This is another shochu from the small islands that trail south of the city (cf. Gojinka Imo from the potato shochu section), and it happens to be from my favorite one, Niijima. I try to spend a few nights there every summer, and I make sure to try one of the great offerings from Miyahara Shuzō each time. This is their regular *mugi* shochu except that it's aged in American Oak and sherry casks. Drink it either *oyuwari* or *nurukan* to really draw out the sweetness and aromas from the 100% domestic barley base, but it's also enjoyable with ice. Interestingly, Miyahara Shuzō was formerly a nihonshu brewery.

Rice (*kome*) shochu

Ginka Torikai (吟香 鳥飼 / ぎんか
とりかい) Torikai Shuzō, Kumamoto
Prefecture, Japan
ABV: 25%, *Kōji*: rice (yellow *kōji kin*)
Distillation: low pressure
Recommended serving style:
    Neat   **Rocks**
    Mizuwari   *Oyuwari*

Comments: This rice shochu can be found everywhere, and it's an interesting example of how some examples of the variety can now imitate the white flower, *ginjō* aromas in nihonshu. Torikai is made using the highly-coveted, and expensive, nihonshu rice (*sakamai*) known as Yamada Nishiki. It fits in appropriately any time before or during a meal, and it pairs easily with sushi and *oden*. You might also try it alongside grilled chicken (*yakitori*) or a lightly sweet dessert such as almond tofu (*annindōfu*). Torikai is at its best when it's cold, so if you plan to sip it straight, then chill the bottle beforehand. On the rocks you may find a faint mineral highlight at the finish. Don't drink Torikai *oyuwari* though because it tends to accent the alcohol at the expense of the fruit notes. By the way, it's pronounced 'Ginka', not 'Ginkō.' Many establishments and publications in Japan use the wrong pronunciation, but I called the distillery and checked, so take my word for it.

Hakutake Shiro (白岳 しろ / はくた
け しろ) Takahashi Shuzō, Kumamoto
Prefecture, Japan
ABV: 25%, *Kōji*: rice (white *kōji kin*)
Distillation: low pressure
Recommended serving style:
  Neat   **Rocks**
  Mizuwari   *Oyuwari*

Comments: Shiro is a very light and easy-sipping *kome* shochu
thanks to the use of low pressure distillation. It's the simplest
and softest of the bottles in this section, if not the entire chapter.
There are lots of pairing possibilities here, such as smoked
salmon or cheese. Much like Ginka Torikai, I recommend
keeping the bottle chilled in case you might want to enjoy it
neat.

Sennen Nebosuke (千年 寝坊助 / せ
んねん ねぼすけ) Kenjō Co., Fukuoka
Prefecture, Japan
ABV: 25%, Koji: rice (yellow *kōji kin*)
Distillation: low pressure
Recommended serving style:

<u>**Neat**</u>	<u>**Rocks**</u>
Mizuwari	*Oyuwari*

Comments: This is an easy to drink, light on the attack, rice
shochu. A crowd pleaser with its adorable label, the name of
this shochu can loosely be translated to 'overslept for a thousand
years.' It can be paired well with fried food and barbecued
meats. As with the other rice shochu in this section, it tastes
best at lower temperatures, and I usually drink it on the rocks.

Awamori

Kiku no Tsuyu (菊之露 / きく の つゆ)
Kikunotsuyu Shuzō, Okinawa Prefecture,
Japan
ABV: 30%, *Kōji*: rice (black *kōji kin*)
Distillation: atmospheric pressure
Recommended serving style:
    Neat   **Rocks**
    Mizuwari   *Oyuwari*

Comments: This is a smooth awamori from Miyakojima, a
beautiful dab of land that is home to a total of seven Awamori
distilleries if you count the two on the satellite island of Irabu.
In addition to the most popular serving style, *mizuwari*, I
highly recommend trying it *oyuwari*—especially if you reside
in a more temperate climate. Keep in mind, however, that this
is a 30% ABV spirit we're dealing with here, so it is perhaps
prudent to alter the ratio a bit. Maybe 4:6 (awamori: hot water)
is a good starting point, and then adjust according to taste.
Another way to enjoy awamori in the summer is to plop a lime
wedge down in the bottom of a cocktail glass, throw some ice
on top of it, and then fill with awamori.

Kumesen (久米仙 / くめせん) Kumesen
Shuzō, Okinawa Prefecture, Japan
ABV: 30%, *Kōji*: rice (black *kōji kin*)
Distillation: atmospheric pressure
Recommended serving style:

Neat	**Rocks**
Mizuwari	*Oyuwari*

Comments: This awamori starts off with a citrusy fragrance, and you'll find that it's medium-bodied and slightly sweet when you first take a sip. However, depending on how cold you've made it, you'll find that the sweetness gives way to a refreshing dryness. Pair this with red meat and even tofu dishes. Enjoyable either on the rocks or with several splashes of water, be careful not to get it mixed up with another delicious awamori, Kumejima Kumesen.

Zuisen (瑞泉 / ずいせん) Zuisen Shuzō,
Okinawa Prefecture, Japan
ABV: 30-31%, *Kōji*: rice (black *kōji kin*)
Distillation: atmospheric pressure
Recommended serving style:

Neat	**Rocks**
Mizuwari	*Oyuwari*

Comments: This awamori presents itself with a sweet, almost brown sugar nose. But you may find that it's drier than the aromas lead you to suspect. I think that Zuisen is best enjoyed on the rocks, but it should also keep people very happy in a tried-and-true *mizuwari* mix. Awamori in general, and Zuisen in particular, pairs nicely with Chinese food, and it goes without saying that it's a safe bet any time you're eating *gōya chanpurū*.

Brown sugar (*kokutō*) shochu

Asahi (朝日 / あさひ) Asahi Shuzō, Kagoshima Prefecture, Japan
ABV: 30%, *Kōji*: rice (white *kōji kin*)
Distillation: atmospheric pressure
Recommended serving style:

Neat	**Rocks**
Mizuwari	***Oyuwari***

Comments: Medium-bodied with a clean finish, this *kokutō* shochu does a good job of balancing its caramel sweetness with a warm richness of flavor. Asahi is tank-aged and works well as an accompaniment to creamy pastas or cheese fondue. You know that tomato and mozzarella slices with basil leaves and olive oil appetizer that appears everywhere during summer months? Try a glass of Asahi alongside it.

Mankoi (まんこい) Yayoi Shochu Jōzōjo, Kagoshima Prefecture, Japan
ABV: 30%, *Kōji*: rice (white *kōji kin*)
Distillation: atmospheric pressure
Recommended serving style:
Neat   <u>**Rocks**</u>
<u>Mizuwari</u>   *Oyuwari*

Comments: This beautiful shochu is cask-aged for at least three years before bottling, and it has a mellow attack that rounds into warm hints of rum. It's a complex shochu that is nonetheless very easy to handle thanks to the extended time that it spent sleeping in an oak barrel. For me, this drink has the swagger to follow a savory meal, and it's excellent slightly chilled in a brandy snifter.

Sango (珊瑚 / さんご) Nishihira Shuzō, Kagoshima Prefecture, Japan
ABV: 30%, *Kōji*: rice (white *kōji kin*)
Distillation: atmospheric pressure
Recommended serving style:
    Neat   **Rocks**
    Mizuwari   *Oyuwari*

Comments: Sango, which means coral in Japanese, is another offering from the beautiful, secluded islands that stretch south from Kagoshima proper toward the tropical paradise of Okinawa. This lace of islands is known as Amami, and it's the only region where *kokutō* shochu is made. Sango, for its part, is tank-aged for a year which is why it lacks color, unlike its barrel-aged brethren. The result is a very dry shochu that doesn't have as much sweetness as you might expect. It is tasty *oyuwari*, but try it on the rocks or *mizuwari* first. And don't neglect to savor the rum notes on the nose before partaking.

Other

Aloe (*aroe*) shochu

Asa no Shizuku (朝 の 雫 / あ さ の し ず
く) Hana no Tsuyu, Fukuoka Prefecture,
Japan
ABV: 23%, *Kōji*: rice (*kōji kin* type
unknown)
Distillation: unknown
Recommended serving style:

| **Neat** | **Rocks** |
| *Mizuwari* | *Oyuwari* |

Comments: The aloe used here is sourced from Okinawa
Prefecture, and the rice strain used in the *kōji* is actually the
same high quality *kome* used in many fine nihonshu, Yamada
Nishiki. There's a very light butterscotch quality in the nose
if you take just half a whiff. It's a very smooth shochu that
will remind you of rice but with fleeting bitter accents and a
resulting refreshing quality. This is a good choice for before a
meal or a Sunday afternoon out on the patio.

Buckwheat (*soba*) shochu

Unkai (雲海 / うんかい) Unkai Shuzō, Miyazaki Prefecture, Japan
ABV: 25%, *Kōji*: barley (white *kōji kin*)
Distillation: low pressure
Recommended serving style:
  Neat   **Rocks**
  Mizuwari ***Oyuwari***

Comments: This is a very tasty buckwheat shochu that I hope you can get your hands on at some point. Buckwheat is what *soba* noodles are made from. Unkai is a refreshing use of that grain and has found widespread popularity in Japan after hitting the market in 1973. The buckwheat aromas give way to a sweetness that belies the barley and rice used during fermentation. I prefer to drink this one on the rocks because it drops the sweetness just a tad, but you should also try it *oyuwari* for a drier finish. Unkai is a light and refreshing spirit that is often a good starting point for shochu beginners.

Chestnut (*kuri*) shochu

Sannen Koshu (三然 古酒 / さんね
ん こしゅ) Nishiyama Shuzō, Hyōgo
Prefecture, Japan
ABV: 25%, *Kōji*: rice (*kōji kin* type
unknown)
Distillation: unknown
Recommended serving style:
> **Neat**   **Rocks**
> *Mizuwari*   *Oyuwari*

Comments: At least 50% of the weight of this shochu's
ingredients are chestnuts, and it's aged for more than three
years in oak barrels. Perhaps the most interesting piece of the
drink's story is exactly where it's stored—the distillery uses
an abandoned train tunnel to let it mature at a constant cool
temperature (10 degrees Celsius). From nose to finish, the
chestnuts are firmly in command on this one, but there's also
a complimenting influence from the oak which adds depth to
the sweetness. This shochu finishes softly after flaring some
post-attack red fruit.

Green pepper (*pīman*) shochu

Piment (ぴめんと) Ochiai Shuzōjo, Miyazaki Prefecture, Japan
ABV: 25%, *Kōji*: rice (white *kōji kin*)
Distillation: unknown
Recommended serving style:
    Neat   **<u>Rocks</u>**
    <u>Mizuwari</u> *Oyuwari*

Comments: This is a (green?) bell pepper shochu and another example of how English spellings can go a little awry. It says 'Piment' on the bottle, but it really should have an 'o' on the end because that's how it's pronounced in Japanese. On the back of the bottle it is mentioned that the inspiration for the name of this shochu was the Spanish word for pepper, 'pimiento', in which case they forgot two vowels plus the fact that pimientos are generally red. Whatever. I'm including this bottle here because it was a happy discovery for me, and you'll enjoy the interplay of citrus and tangy notes. The pepper doesn't blast away on the nose, but it comes through unmistakably on the palate.

Perilla (*shiso*) shochu

Tantakatan (鍛高譚 / たんたかたん)
Oenon Group, Tokyo, Japan
ABV: 20%, *Kōji*: unknown
Distillation: unknown
Recommended serving style:

Neat	**Rocks**
Mizuwari	*Oyuwari*

Comments: This shochu is not actually honkaku, but I've included it because I've met several people from a variety of countries who quite like it. This is a blended (*konwa*) shochu, 88% *kōrui* (multiple-distilled) and 12% *otsurui* (single-distilled). In addition to *shiso*, sometimes referred to as basil's Asian cousin, dates are added to the fermentation. It's a simple, refreshing tipple that is easy to drink and best consumed on the rocks or with cool water. Avoid hot water with Tantakatan as an *oyuwari* mix can blow the *shiso* notes out of proportion. The production process has largely been kept a secret, so it's the only bottle in this chapter for which both the type of *kōji* and distillation method remain a mystery to the general public.

Sesame (*goma*) shochu

Beni Otome (べに 乙女 / べに おとめ)
Beni Otome Shuzō, Fukuoka Prefecture, Japan
ABV: 25%, *Kōji*: rice (white *kōji kin*)
Distillation: low pressure
Recommended serving style:

Neat	**Rocks**
Mizuwari	*Oyuwari*

Comments: According to the label, sesame makes up at least 20% of the ingredients used to make this drink. In addition to the sesame and rice, barley is used to help round this tank-aged shochu out. The sesame is very apparent in the bouquet—quite similar to the complexity found in sesame oil and deepened by a whiff of steamed potatoes. Grilled sesame seeds come through on the palate, as does a late-arriving almost walnutty bitterness. If quieting the sesame down a little is what you're after, then drink this one on the rocks. Drinking it *oyuwari*, on the other hand, will draw out the umami.

Chapter 9
Shochu recipes

Cocktails
If you're the type that trends towards mixology, then this chapter is for you. The first half contains recipes for shochu cocktails, and the second half details liqueurs that you can make in the comfort of your own home.

Using multiple-distilled *kōrui* shochu is the best bet for the following cocktail recipes. However, you can also use a light honkaku barley shochu such as *Iichiko* in many cases. A relatively nondescript rice shochu like *Hakutake Shiro* (see chapter eight) should also work. Keep in mind that because *kōrui* shochu has a lower ABV (25 or 35%, depending on the variety) than vodka or gin, these will be slightly milder and have fewer calories than what you may be used to.

Shochu Highball (*chūhai*)
Ingredients:
  kōrui shochu
  club soda
  lemon wedge

Add ice to a tumbler or highball glass, and fill one-third to one-half of the glass with *kōrui* shochu. Fill the rest of the glass with club soda. Garnish with lemon, grapefruit, or other fruit of your choice.

Shochu and Cola (*kolawari*)
Ingredients:
  kōrui shochu
  cola
  lemon slice

Add ice to a tumbler or highball glass, and fill one-third to one-half of the glass with *kōrui* shochu. Top up with cola and garnish with a slice of lemon. The cola can easily be switched with ginger ale.

Shochu Driver
Ingredients:
  kōrui shochu
  orange juice

Add ice to a tumbler or highball glass, and fill one-third to one-half of the glass with *kōrui* shochu. Fill the rest of the way with orange juice. Stir and serve.

Shochu Alaska
Ingredients:
  kōrui shochu
  orange bitters
  Yellow Chartreuse
  lemon peel twist

Add two parts *kōrui* shochu and one part Yellow Chartreuse to a shaker. Add a couple drops of orange bitters and ice cubes as well. Shake and strain into a cocktail glass with a lemon peel twist.

Shochu Alexander
Ingredients:
  kōrui shochu
  coffee liqueur
  crème de cacao
  cream

Add one part each of coffee liqueur, crème de cacao, and cream to a cocktail shaker with ice. Add three parts *kōrui* shochu as well. Shake and strain into a cocktail glass. Enjoy.

Shochu Bloody Mary
Ingredients:
  kōrui shochu
  tomato juice
  hot sauce (2-4 dashes)
  Worcestershire sauce (dash)
  salt (pinch)
  pepper (pinch)
  lemon juice
  celery stick

Throw everything but the celery stick into a shaker or mixing glass. One part *kōrui* shochu, half as much lemon juice, and three parts tomato juice. Add ice cubes to a large glass and strain the mixture over the top. Garnish with a celery stick and serve.

Shochu White Russian
Ingredients:
  kōrui shochu
  coffee liqueur
  light cream

Pour two parts *kōrui* shochu and one part coffee liqueur over ice in an old-fashioned glass. Fill the rest of the way with light cream and serve. You can also use milk in place of the light cream.

Chū Tonic
Ingredients:
    kōrui shochu
    tonic water

Add ice to a tumbler or highball glass, and fill one-third to one-half of the glass with *kōrui* shochu. Top up with tonic water, garnish with a lime wedge, and serve.

Salty Shochu Dog
Ingredients:
    kōrui shochu
    grapefruit juice
    salt

Add equal parts *kōrui* shochu and grapefruit juice to an ice-filled shaker. Strain into a salt-rimmed, ice-filled glass. Drink.

Green Shochu
Ingredients:
    kōrui shochu
    Lemon-Lime Kool-Aid mix
    Sprite

Drop one part *kōrui* shochu, two parts Sprite, and plenty of Kool-Aid powder in a cocktail shaker with a bit of ice. Shake like crazy, and then pour over rocks in a tumbler.

Note: A good option for St. Patrick's Day. 7-Up will also work.

Shochu Martini
Ingredients:
  kōrui shochu
  dry vermouth
  green olive

In a mixing glass with ice cubes, pour three parts *kōrui* shochu and a splash or two of dry vermouth. Stir the mixture like you mean it. Strain into a cocktail glass and drop the green olive in there. Instead of the olive, you can also spruce this up with a lemon rind twist. Also, chilling the cocktail glass beforehand will increase enjoyment.

Shochu Cosmopolitan
Ingredients:
  kōrui shochu
  Cointreau
  cranberry juice
  lime

Add ice to a cocktail shaker, and drench with one part *kōrui* shochu, half as much Cointreau, one part cranberry juice, and the juice from half of a lime. Shake until your hands are frozen. Serve in a cocktail glass with a lime slice as garnish.

The Makarim
Ingredients:
  2 oz. Bombay Sapphire gin
  1 oz. brown sugar umeshu
  1 oz. *Momo* no *Kuchidoke* peach liqueur
  2 oz. lemon soda water

Add everything except for the soda to an ice-filled shaker. Cover and pulverize the contents. Uncover and add the lemon soda water, stirring gently. Strain into a large martini glass, and garnish with a lemon twist.

Note: This drink was inspired by a close friend, Mac, and neither he nor the drink should be trifled with. You can split it between two smaller martini glasses if you feel intimidated. Both the umeshu and peach liqueur are made with shochu.

Homemade liqueurs

Homemade creations such as the ones described in this section are exceedingly common in Japan. Supermarkets and home improvement shops almost always have the provisions necessary for creating your own liqueurs, and the health benefits of drinking the fruits of your labor are rumored to run the gamut from stress reduction to putting a little hop in your step. I have found that there are few gifts finer than a bottle filled with a homemade liqueur. It doesn't matter whether it's a dinner party or a house-warming, you'll always put a smile on the recipient's face. However, please bear in mind that it is illegal in many jurisdictions to sell any macerated delights that you create.

Large mason jars are best for this kind of hobby. Anything that's a liter or larger is perfect, and if it has a gasket then that's fantastic. However, any kind of stopper, cap, or cover will do. The most important thing is to keep bacteria and other nasties out of the mixture while it matures. If you don't have any large jars, then dividing the ingredients between four or more pint-sized jars will also work. The other tools that you'll need are probably already available in your home. A cutting board, paring knife, and strainers of different sizes will come in handy, as will a large bowl, measuring cup, cheesecloth, and funnel. A kitchen scale and perhaps a single cup coffee filter holder with paper filters would be a nice bonus if you have them lying around. You'll eventually need an empty wine bottle or something of a similar stature, plus *kōrui* shochu. The wine bottle needs to be completely clean and dry when you strain the finished macerated shochu into it. Don't use plastic or any containers that could impart an off taste in your liqueur. Don't use crystal jars with lead in them either (for obvious reasons).

Kōrui shochu (35% ABV) is the safest bet here thanks to its pure palate, but you can also create some delicious libations using a light barley or rice shochu. Barrel-aged shochu could also be fun to try with a variety of sweet and spicy ingredients, or perhaps even herbs. It's also possible to add wine or other spirits to your creations to take the flavors in a new direction—you're truly only limited by your imagination.

Rock sugar is reportedly better than regular white sugar because it dissolves more slowly, but if you can't find it at your local specialty or Asian market, then the regular stuff should work just fine. Also, pay close attention to the recommended steeping times for each recipe. Time directly correlates with intensity in the world of maceration. That said, 35% alcohol will not strip the flavors from the other ingredients as quickly as a higher ABV spirit, so don't be afraid to taste the mixture periodically and let it "marry" a bit longer if you aren't yet happy with the intensity of the flavor. If you're making a fruit liqueur, then you can speed things up by using frozen fruit. Frozen generally beats fresh in terms of sweetness, believe it or not, and that's why pastry chefs often opt for the icy stuff.

Finally, rock the jar gently every day to make sure that the ingredients blend smoothly. The resulting creations will allow you to add a new twist to martinis and countless other cocktails. Start by trying a couple of the simple recipes here, and then branch off into uncharted territory when you feel like you have the hang of it.

Rosemary Shochu
Ingredients:
    kōrui shochu - 350 ml
    red wine - 350 ml
    fresh rosemary - 40 g
    rock sugar - 50 g

Wash the rosemary thoroughly and add it to the jar along with the sugar. Pour the red wine and *kōrui* shochu over the top and seal the container. Agitate gently and store in a cool, dark place for one week. Use a coffee filter-lined funnel to strain the contents into a wine bottle.

Note: This liqueur can be paired with meat dishes and is best enjoyed on the rocks or *mizuwari*. Also, thyme or sage can be substituted for the rosemary in this recipe. Sage also goes well with meat dishes, but thyme is probably best paired with fish.

Ginger Shochu
Ingredients:
    kōrui shochu - 700 ml
    fresh ginger - 150 g

Wash the raw ginger thoroughly and carve out any blemishes. Slice the ginger thinly and then drop the slices in the bottom of the jar. Submerge the ginger slices in *kōrui* shochu, and seal the jar. Store out of sunlight in a cool part of your home for two months. Use a coffee filter-lined funnel to strain the contents into a wine bottle.

Note: I recommend drinking this *oyuwari* when it's cold outside. Add some honey to taste; this is a nice treat after dinner. It pairs well with stir-fried dishes and can also be enjoyed on the rocks. It's also rumored to fight against hangovers.

Cinnamon Shochu
Ingredients:
kōrui shochu - 900 ml
cinnamon chunks - 25 g

Drop the cinnamon chunks in the jar and pour *kōrui* shochu over them. Seal the jar and store in a cool, dark place for three weeks. Use a coffee filter-lined funnel to strain the contents into a wine bottle.

Note: Cinnamon shochu liqueur is nice either neat or on the rocks. Alternatively, add it to coffee for a bit of fun.

Tomato Shochu
Ingredients:
kōrui shochu - 450 ml
tomatoes - 300 g
lemon - 1 whole

Thoroughly wash and dry the tomatoes before halving them and slicing to 1 cm thickness. Peel the lemon, slice, and add all of the sliced fruit to the jar. Pour *kōrui* shochu over the ingredients. Seal the container and allow to rest in a cool, dark place for at least one month. Use a coffee filter-lined funnel to strain the contents into a wine bottle.

Note: Enjoy this liqueur straight, on the rocks, or in cocktail using vegetable juice.

Strawberry Shochu
Ingredients:
kōrui shochu - 600 ml
strawberries - 300 g
lemon - 1 whole
rock sugar - 50 g

Stem and halve the strawberries before thoroughly washing them. Remove any excess water, and then add them to the jar with the peeled, thinly sliced lemon and sugar. Pour the *kōrui* shochu over the bed of ingredients and seal the container. Agitate lightly and store in a cool place away from light for two weeks. Use a coffee filter-lined funnel to strain the contents into a wine bottle.

Notes: Strawberry shochu liqueur is delicious on the rocks and can even be poured over pound cake or ice cream. Kiwis, apples, or blueberries can also be used in this recipe instead of strawberries. Both the kiwi and apple versions are nice with soda water. The blueberry option would be good mixed with ice cream or yogurt. All three of these alternatives must macerate for two months before filtering. Cranberries can also be used, but rather than the 300 g prescribed above, reduce the amount to 200 g. Cranberry shochu liqueur pairs well with chicken dishes.

Autumn Apple Shochu
Ingredients:
   kōrui shochu - 500 ml
   brandy - 250 ml
   apples - 1 kg
   cinnamon - 3 sticks

Stem and wash the apples thoroughly. After drying them, slice into eighths and add to the jar with the cinnamon sticks. Pour the brandy and *kōrui* shochu over the top, and then seal the jar. Store in a cool, dark area of your home for six weeks. Use a coffee filter-lined funnel to strain the contents into a wine bottle.

Note: Simple syrup can be added at bottling to sweeten the taste. Also, since the apples will hold on to a fair amount of alcohol, put them in a plastic bag, crush them, and then filter the juice into the bottle.

Bacon Shochu
Ingredients:
    kōrui shochu - 700 ml
    bacon - 4 thick strips

Cook the bacon in a frying pan and add it to the jar along with the drippings. Pour the *kōrui* shochu over the top and seal the jar. Place the jar in the freezer for two hours. Use a coffee filter-lined funnel to strain the contents into a wine bottle. This should filter out most of the hardened drippings.

Note: Filter a second or third time for increased clarity. If you *really* like bacon, then leave the jar in the freezer for up to a whole day. This value-added shochu will contribute a totally new dimension to your home bar.

Candy Corn Shochu
Ingredients:
    kōrui shochu - 700 ml
    candy corns - 500 g

Put the candy corns in the jar. Pour the *kōrui* shochu over the top and seal the jar. Place the jar in a cool, dark place for one week. Gently shake the jar once a day to help the flavors mix. Strain into a bottle.

Note: This is one brightly-colored shochu! Coffee filters will remove some of the color, so you may want to use a mesh strainer when funneling it into the bottle. Jelly beans also work well with this simple recipe. This is the perfect base for Candy Corn Shochu Martinis at a Halloween party.

Cucumber Shochu
Ingredients:
    kōrui shochu - 750 ml
    cucumber - 300 g

Wash and peel the cucumbers. Slice them and put them in the jar. Pour the *kōrui* shochu over the bed of cucumber slices and seal the jar. Store the jar in a cool, dark place for two weeks. Use a coffee filter-lined funnel to strain the contents into a wine bottle.

Note: This is a refreshing drink that will work nicely with the cosmopolitan and martini recipes from the cocktail section of this chapter. Alternatively, serve on the rocks with a fish dinner.

Vanilla Shochu
Ingredients:
    kōrui shochu - 750 ml
    vanilla beans - 2 whole

Wash the beans thoroughly and pat dry. Cut the beans open, but don't slice them in half. Drop the beans in the jar and submerge them with the *kōrui* shochu. Let the beans macerate for 10 days in a cool, dark area of your home. Use a coffee filter-lined funnel to strain the contents into a wine bottle.

Note: Taste this mixture daily after one week, and filter it into a bottle when it's the right intensity for you. If you really love the taste of vanilla, then don't be afraid to let the beans macerate for two weeks or longer.

Umeshu
Ingredients:
  kōrui shochu
  green *ume* "plums"
  rock sugar

Three year old homemade umeshu.

The exact amount of each ingredient will depend on the size of your jar. You will need enough *ume* (pronounced /u meh/) to fill the jar half way. You will also need between one-quarter and one-half as much rock sugar as the weight of green *ume*. In other words, if one kilo of *ume* fills the jar half way, then you'll need 250-500 g of rock sugar.

Rip the deep stems out of the *ume*, wash them thoroughly, and pat dry. Make one layer of *ume* on the bottom of the infusion jar, and pour a thin bed of rock sugar over the top of it. Repeat with alternating layers of fruit and rock sugar until you run out of the former. Pour the *kōrui* shochu over the top until the surface of the alcohol is 5-10 cm above the layered bed of *ume* and sugar. Store in a cool, dark part of your home for at least three months. Occasionally stir or rock the infusion gently so that the sugar and alcohol are recombined.

Note: This is perhaps the most common type of liqueur made at home in Japan, and a brown sugar version features in The Makarim cocktail recipe above. The bigger your infusion jar, the better (I use a three liter jar when I make it). The contents are fine to drink after three months, but the drink will mature significantly over a full year of maceration. At one year, strain the infusion into a bottle. Serve neat, on the rocks, or with soda water. Oh, and *ume* aren't really plums. They're actually more closely related to apricots, but whatever.

Chapter 10
Basic Japanese for shochu drinkers

This chapter is designed to provide linguistic assistance to those lucky folks who will have a chance to visit Japan and enjoy shochu in its native environment. Here you will find simple Japanese expressions with their rough English equivalents and basic pronunciation patterns. Fortunately for the English speakers of the world, it is not difficult to fairly accurately replicate the pronunciation of most Japanese words simply by looking at an English representation of it. There are only five vowel sounds, and there's a lot of overlap with those of the Spanish and Italian languages.

Pronunciation
One important difference, however, is that Japanese is a syllable-timed language, rather than a stress-timed language like English. What I mean by this is that each syllable in a Japanese word should be given equal weight and length, and individual words should not be stressed unless you're trying to draw attention to a specific idea. As with any language, however, there are a few exceptions that you'll need to keep in mind when using the transliterated Japanese words either in conversation or when ordering a drink. In this book I have adhered, more or less, to the rules of Revised Hepburn Romanization for Japanese.

Although vowel sounds can stand alone, syllables are normally comprised of two parts—a consonant followed by a vowel. Consonants never follow vowels, unless you include those instances when you see 'n' at the end of a syllable or word. That 'n' is actually not a consonant, it's a nasalization of the vowel to its left and can present orally as either an [m] or [n] sound depending on the first sound of the following syllable.

Another trick to keep in mind is that consonant sounds can change in certain situations. I'm not going to get into the details here, but the gist of the matter is that unvoiced consonants occasionally become voiced. For instance, *h*, *k*, *s*, and *t* are sometimes rendered as *b*, *g*, *z*, and *d*, respectively. This can clearly be seen when comparing the words sushi and *makizushi*.

An especially important pronunciation foible for readers of this book to keep in mind is that, even though I have consistently written shochu as fronted by an *sh* consonant, it's not always spoken that way. When the word shochu is preceded by the name of the main ingredient, it's likely that Japanese speakers will change the *sh* to a *j* sound. In other words, *imo* shochu becomes *imo* jochu, and *mugi* shochu is often pronounced *mugi* jochu in conversation.

One final thing to pay attention to when dealing with Romanized versions of Japanese words is elongated vowels. Any time you see a macron above a vowel (usually ō or ū), you would need to extend the length of the syllable when saying it aloud. The macrons have been included here purely for academic accuracy, but it's actually uncommon to see them used in daily life. Also, as mentioned at the beginning of this book, I have removed macrons from Japanese words that have been (or will be) borrowed as-is by English speakers. Proper nouns have also been rendered macron-less. So even though you will consistently encounter *kōji* and *kokutō* in this book, remember that they are more commonly found in the wild without macrons as *koji* and *kokuto*.

Here are the five vowel sounds found in Japanese along with their approximations in English:

Japanese vowel - English equivalent

a - *ah* as in father (NOT like the *a* in man)

e - *eh* as in get (NOT like the *e* in recede)

i - *ee* as in tree or we (NOT like the *i* in tricycle or trip)

o - *oh* as in zone (NOT like the *o* in on or won)

u - *u* as in glue (NOT like *u* in fun)

Using the English equivalents of the vowel sounds listed above, here is how some of the usual suspects from this book would look from a more pronunciation-oriented perspective. It's not normal for the words to be transliterated in this fashion, but it might help if you've never heard spoken Japanese before. I've added spaces to break up the syllables, but remember that they should all receive equal weight or stress when spoken out loud. Check the glossary for extra practice pronouncing Japanese shochu-related words.

honkaku - /hohn kah ku/
shochu - /shōh chū/
kōrui - /kōh ru ee/
kōji - /kōh jee/
imo - /ee moh/
mugi - /mu gee/

kome - /koh meh/
awamori - /ah wah moh ree/
kokutō - /koh ku tōh/

Useful Japanese phrases
Market / Liquor shop

Almost every supermarket, convenience store, and bottle shop in Japan has at least a modest selection of shochu, so the number of expressions needed is relatively small. Supermarket and liquor store staff generally won't approach you like employees in Japanese department, clothing, or electronics stores tend to. Instead, it's highly likely that you'll need to track someone down. You may find that some of the expressions from the *Restaurant / Bar / Izakaya* section come in handy as well.

The expressions are further organized according to linguistic themes, primarily the verbs that are used and any other patterns that might make the phrases easier to commit to memory. Each entry begins with the Japanese version and is followed by an English translation. I have included a *kana* representation of each expression that includes spaces corresponding to the Romanized rendering that follows.

すみません。(*Sumimasen.*)
Excuse me (see Note 1 in the next section)

本格焼酎はどこですか。(ほんかく しょうちゅう は ど こ です か。/ Honkaku shochu *wa doko desu ka?*)
Where is the honkaku shochu?

どれは本格焼酎ですか。(どれ は ほんかく しょうちゅ う です か。/ *Dore wa* honkaku shochu *desu ka?*)
Which one(s) is/are honkaku shochu?

Restaurant / Bar / Izakaya
Here are some general expressions that you can use to navigate a dining/bar experience in Japanese. Underlined words can be substituted with the words that follow.

A hole-in-the-wall shochu bar in Kagoshima city.

何名様ですか。 (なん めい さま です か。/ *Nan mei sama desu ka?*)
How many people in your party?
一人です。 (ひとり です。/ *Hitori desu.*)—A table for <u>one</u>, please.
二人 (ふたり / *futari*) 三人 (さん にん / *san nin*)—two-three
四人 (よ にん / *yo nin*) 五人 (ご にん / *go nin*)—four-five
六人 (ろく にん / *roku nin*) 七人 (なな にん / *nana nin*)—six-seven
八人 (はち にん / *hachi nin*) 九人 (きゅう にん / *kyū nin*)—eight-nine
十人 (じゅう にん / *jū nin*)—ten

<u>禁煙席</u>お願いします。 (<u>きんえん せき</u> おねがい します。/ <u>*Kin'en seki*</u> *onegai shimasu.*)
<u>Non-smoking seat</u>, please.

メニュー (めにゅー / *Me'nyū*)
Menu

飲み物メニュー (のみもの めにゅー / *Nomimono me'nyū*)
Drink menu

お会計 (おかいけい / *Okaikei*)
Check

Note 1: ...*onegai shimasu* is one of the magic Japanese phrases that you absolutely must memorize. You can put almost any noun phrase in front of it, including destinations when taking a cab, and the result is a polite request. Alternatively, "*Onegai shimasu*" can be substituted for "*Sumimasen*" from the Market / Liquor Shop section as a way to get someone's attention. It takes a little getting used to, but don't be afraid to call these expressions out if the place is hopping or for whatever reason there's no server in sight.

Note 2: Also, rather than a table charge, many izakaya and bars will give each person in your party a small dish of food shortly after sitting down. This is called *otōshi* (お通し / おとおし), and you should expect to see a charge for it on the bill.

ありがとうございます。 (*Arigatō gozaimasu*.)
Thank you.

Note 3: Memorize this one, too. If you want to sound even more polite, add the word *dōmo* (どうも) to the beginning.

はい。 / いいえ。 (*Hai*. / *Īe*.)
Yes. / No.

お冷やください。 (おひや ください。 / *Ohiya kudasai*.)
Please give me cold drinking water.
    焼酎 (しょうちゅう / shochu)—shochu
    お湯 (おゆ / *oyu*)—hot water
    お水 (おみず / *omizu*)—water (cold)
    氷 (こおり / *kōri*)—ice
    お箸 (おはし / *ohashi*)—chopsticks
    スプーン (すぷーん / *supūn*)—spoon
    フォーク (ふぉーく / *fōku*)—fork
    取り皿 (とりざら / *torizara*)—small plate/dish
    おしぼり (*oshibori*)—wet towel
    これ (*kore*)—this one
    それ (*sore*)—that (near)
    あれ (*are*)—that (far)

Note 4: Menus in Japan often have pictures to aid selection, so pointing while saying *kore kudasai* can get you a long way. Also, don't be shocked if the wait staff or bartender points to something on the menu with their middle finger. They are simply using the longest finger on the human hand, and it's not meant to be offensive. It's actually a logical finger choice for indicating when you think about it.

芋焼酎をロックで一つください。 (いも しょうちゅう を ろっく で ひとつ ください。/ *Imo* shochu *o rokku de hitotsu kudasai.*)

Please give me <u>one</u> potato shochu on the rocks.

Counters for drinks and food

一つ (ひとつ / *hitotsu*) 二つ (ふたつ / *futatsu*)—one-two

三つ (みっつ / *mittsu*) 四つ (よっつ / *yottsu*)—three-four

五つ (いつつ / *itsutsu*) 六つ (むっつ / *muttsu*)—five-six

七つ (ななつ / *nanatsu*) 八つ (やっつ / *yattsu*)—seven-eight

Note 5: Replace the word *rokku* with your preferred serving style: neat (*sutorēto*), cool water mix (*mizuwari*), warm water mix (*nurukan*), or hot water mix (*oyuwari*). Also, a doubled 'k' or 't'—as in the words *rokku* and *mittsu* above—implies an elongated consonant when saying the word. In practice, this equates to inserting a brief glottal stop before the doubled consonant.

とりあえず生。 (とりあえず なま。 / *Toriaezu nama.*)

Let's start with a draft beer.

乾杯！(かんぱい！/ *Kanpai!*)
Cheers!

これは何ですか。(これ は なん です か。/ *Kore wa nan desu ka?*)
What is this?

牛肉は食べられません。(ぎゅうにく は たべられません。/ *Gyūniku wa taberaremasen.*)
I cannot eat <u>beef</u>.
　　豚肉 (ぶた にく / *buta niku*)—pork
　　卵 (たまご / *tamago*)—egg
　　貝類 (かいるい / *kairui*)—shellfish
　　刺身 (さしみ / *sashimi*)—sashimi (raw fish)

ベジタリアンです。(べじたりあん です。/ *Bejitarian desu.*)
I'm (she's/he's) a vegetarian.

牛乳は飲めません。(ぎゅうにゅう は のめません。/ *Gyūnyū wa nomemasen.*)
I cannot drink <u>milk</u>.
　　ウィスキー (うぃすきー / *uisukī*)—whiskey
　　ビール (びーる / *bīru*)—beer
　　日本酒 (にほんしゅ / *nihonshu*)—nihonshu (saké)
　　もう (*mō*)—anymore (drop the '*wa*' after '*mō*')

本格焼酎を飲みたいです。(ほんかく しょうちゅう を のみたい です。/ <u>Honkaku</u> shochu *o nomitai desu.*)
I want to drink <u>honkaku</u> shochu.
　　芋 (いも / *imo*)—potato
　　麦 (むぎ / *mugi*)—barley
　　米 (こめ / *kome*)—rice
　　黒糖 (こくとう / *kokutō*)—brown sugar

泡盛 (あわもり / awamori)—awamori (drop the word shochu)

白麹 (しろこうじ / *shiro kōji*)—white *kōji* (plus ingredient)

黒麹 (くろこうじ / *kuro kōji*)—black *kōji* (plus ingredient)

黄麹 (きこうじ / *ki kōji*)—yellow *kōji* (plus ingredient)

おすすめは何ですか。 (おすすめ は なん です か。 / *Osusume wa nan desu ka?*)
What do you recommend?

いくらですか。 / (*Ikura desu ka?*)—How much does it cost?

どれですか。 / (*Dore desu ka?*)—Which one?

お手洗いはどこですか。 (おてあらい は どこ です か。 / *Otearai wa doko desu ka?*)
Where is the restroom/toilet?

おいしいです！ (*Oishī desu!*)
It's delicious!

大丈夫です。 (だいじょうぶ です。 / *Daijōbu desu.*)
It's/I'm OK.

Note 6: This is another essential expression. *Daijōbu* is like the duct tape of the Japanese language—it can be used in a zillion different situations. For example, the above expression can be teamed with appropriate nodding or shaking of the head to mean either yes or no. Add the question particle *-ka* to the end, and you have yourself a very handy question stem.

クレジットカード大丈夫ですか。 (くれじっとかーど だいじょうぶ です か。 / *Kurejitto kādo daijōbu desu ka?*)

Is a <u>credit card</u> OK?

写真 (しゃしん / *shashin*)—photo

靴 (くつ / *kutsu*)—shoes

Note 7: Some izakaya require you to remove your shoes just after coming through the door. A pretty good indication is when there's a standing area just inside the entry, but it's one or two steps down from the floor level of the rest of the place. Another dead giveaway is when you can see a wall of mini lockers with odd wooden or metal 'keys.' When in doubt, just use the above phrase, "*Kutsu daijōbu desu ka?*"

<u>焼酎</u>はありますか。 (<u>しょうちゅう</u> は あります か。 / <u>Shochu</u> *wa arimasu ka*?)

Do you have <u>shochu</u>?

飲み放題 (のみほうだい / *nomihōdai*)—"all you can drink" deal

食べ放題 (たべほうだい / *tabehōdai*)—"all you can eat" deal

Note 8: Some bars and izakaya have timed, limited menu deals where you can drink and/or eat as much as you want for a set price. Don't be surprised if they tell you that it's "last order" when you still have 30 minutes left on the clock. If you want to have another drink after "last order" on the *nomihōdai* menu, then you'll need to order it *tan'pin* which means that you'll pay the regular menu price for it. The same is true for karaoke room *nomihōdai* deals.

Glossary

The vast majority of the entries here are Japanese words that are important to the production, purchase, and appreciation of shochu. Words that are Japanese (and will likely stay that way) are indicated in italicized Revised Hepburn transliteration. Words that will likely gain membership to the English dictionary have the italicized Revised Hepburn reading inside brackets following the Anglicized reading. However, only time will tell. Importantly, I have avoided italicizing locations in this glossary.

A

ABV - Alcohol by volume. Generally preceded by a percentage.

Amami Guntō (奄美 群島 / あまみ ぐんとう) - Amami Islands. An archipelago with eight main inhabited islands that is administratively part of Kagoshima Prefecture despite being geographically far closer to Okinawa. The islands host more than two dozen shochu distilleries, the vast majority of which specialize in producing Amami *Kokutō* Shochu.

Amami *Kokutō* Shochu (奄美 黒糖 焼酎 / あまみ こくとう し ょうちゅう) - Brown sugar shochu that is made exclusively in the Amami Guntō area of Japan. Rice *kōji* is used in the first *moromi* fermentation stage (*ichiji shikomi*). Melted, diluted brown sugar is added to the second *moromi* fermentation (*niji shikomi*).

arak - A word used in parts of the Middle East and Southeast Asia to identify the varied distilled beverages made in those regions. Back during shochu's early days, the drink was sometimes called *araki shu* (阿剌吉酒 or アラキ酒).

Aspergillus awamori - The scientific name for the black mold spores used in the production of awamori and an increasing number of shochu. *Kōji* made using black *kōji kin* is called *kuro kōji*. These mold spores help convert starch to sugar. There is not universal agreement on the correct name for this strain, so it is also called *Awamori luchuensis* by many scientists in Japan.

Aspergillus kawachi kitahara - The scientific name for the white mold spores used to make shochu. This is the most commonly used variant of *Aspergillus* in shochu production. *Kōji* made using white *kōji kin* is called *shiro kōji*. These mold spores help convert starch to sugar. Also known as *Aspergillus kawachii* (two i's), *Aspergillus awamori* var. *kawachi*, and *Aspergillus luchuensis mut. kawachii*.

Aspergillus oryzae - The scientific name for the yellow mold spores used in the brewing of nihonshu and an increasing number of shochu. *Kōji* made using yellow *kōji kin* is called *ki kōji*. These mold spores help convert starch to sugar.

atsukan (熱燗 / あつかん) – Hot alcohol. More often used to refer to very hot nihonshu, but is a serving style for shochu as well.

awamori [*awamori*] (泡盛 / あわもり) - Distilled alcoholic beverage made in the Okinawan Islands. Although it is closely related to shochu, there are several procedural differences such as exclusive use of *indica* rice and black *kōji*, and single mash fermentation (*zenkōji shikomi*). Also known as Ryūkyū Awamori.

B

beni azuma (紅 アズマ / べに あずま) - A variety of sweet potato (*satsuma imo*) that is used in both cooking and shochu production.

beni hayato (紅 ハヤト / べに はやと) - A variety of sweet potato (*satsuma imo*) that is known for having a lot of beta carotene.

beni satsuma (紅 さつま / べに さつま) - Kochi Prefecture's indigenous *tosa beni* sweet potatoes which have been grown in Kagoshima Prefecture soil. Known for being soft and flaky.

bin (瓶 / びん) - Bottle.

butaniku no shōgayaki (豚肉 の 生姜焼き / ぶたにく の しょうがやき) - Pan-fried ginger pork, a tasty izakaya staple, is both simple to make and pairs nicely with a variety of different shochu.

C

chōki chozō (長期 貯蔵 / ちょうき ちょぞう) - If at least 50% of the shochu has been aged for three years or longer, the distiller is allowed to put *chōki chozō* on the label. Alternatively, *koshu* can also be printed on the label.

chūhai (酎ハイ or チュウハイ / ちゅうはい) - A portmanteau of shochu highball, it was originally a popular izakaya cocktail (shochu, soda, and fruit or other juice) in downtown Tokyo. Takara Shuzō brought this drink to the masses by creating the fist canned *chūhai* in 1984.

D

daichi no yume (ダイチ ノ ユメ / だいち の ゆめ) - A variety of sweet potato (*satsuma imo*) that boasts a high starch count and tends to have a strong impact on a shochu's bouquet.

E

Edo (江戸 / えど) - Tokyo's former name which it held until the beginning of the Meiji Restoration in 1868.

F

furigana (振り仮名 / ふりがな) - *Kana* written beside or above *kanji* to show correct pronunciation.

G

gen'atsu (減圧 / げんあつ) - Reduced or low pressure. In the shochu industry, this word refers to low pressure distillation (*gen'atsu jōryū*).

genshu (原酒 / げんしゅ) - Unprocessed and unblended shochu. This word can also be used to describe alcohol such as whiskey or nihonshu that has not been processed.

ginjō (吟醸 / ぎんじょう) - The best grade of nihonshu. Loved for its fruity bouquet.

gō (合 / ごう) - 180 ml measure of shochu or nihonshu commonly served in izakaya and restaurants.

gōya (ゴウヤ / ごうや) - Often translated as bitter melon or bitter gourd, this vine fruit is a fixture of Okinawan cuisine. And yes, it's quite bitter.

gōya chanpurū (ゴウヤ チャンプルー / ごうや ちゃんぷるー) - Okinawan stir fry often made with eggs, tofu, *gōya*, and pork.

H

hanatare (はなたれ) - Also known as *hatsudare* (初垂れ / はつ だれ), this is the first part of the distillate which usually boasts 60-70% ABV. If you find a bottle that claims to be *hanatare*, put it in the freezer and drink it straight or on the rocks (cf. *suedare*).

heikō fukuhakkō (並行 複発酵 / へいこう ふくはっこう) - Multiple parallel fermentation. *Kōji kin* spores and yeast working side-by-side to chop starches into simple sugars (glucose), and then convert those sugars into alcohol and carbon dioxide.

hinohikari (ヒノヒカリ / ひのひかり) - A rice varietal that is native to Kyushu Island and used to make shochu.

hiragana (平仮名 / ひらがな) - A round, cursive-like syllabary used mostly to write native Japanese words. Commonly used in tandem with *kanji* for inflections (cf. *katakana*).

honjōzō (本醸造 / ほんじょうぞう) - High grade of nihonshu which includes brewer's alcohol (*jōzō arukōru*). For every ton of rice used, the brewer is allowed to add up to 116 liters of brewer's alcohol. This maximum limit works out to be about 25% of the total alcohol in the nihonshu.

honkaku shochu [*honkaku shōchū*] (本格 焼酎 / ほんかく しょ うちゅう) - Designation indicating single-distilled shochu that was made using approved ingredients and methods. Awamori is also a type of honkaku shochu, but they are normally given equal billing, as in "honkaku shochu and awamori." The honkaku shochu title was adopted in 1971 to help improve single-distilled shochu's reputation amongst Japanese consumers (cf. shochu and *kōrui* shochu).

I

ichiji shikomi (一次 仕込み / いちじ しこみ) - First *moromi* fermentation. A mixture of *kōji* (rice, barley, potato, etc.), water, and yeast which is typically allowed to ferment for five to eight days. The result is the first *moromi* which will then have the main ingredient of the shochu added to it with more water.

Iki Shochu [*Iki Shōchū* or *Iki Jōchū*] (壱岐 焼酎 / いき しょう ちゅう) - Barley shochu that is made on Nagasaki Prefecture's Iki Island. There are currently about a half dozen distilleries in operation on the island. The shochu must use a 2:1 barley to rice *kōji* ratio during fermentation in order to carry the WTO-protected Iki Shochu appellation.

imo (芋 / いも) - Potato.

indica mai (インディカ 米 / いんでぃか まい) - Long-grain varietals of rice that are generally grown in tropical climates. One strain commonly used in Japan is *Thai mai* which is known for being relatively easy to make *kōji* with. Its use is mandated in awamori production, but it has also found increasing popularity in rice and potato shochu distilleries (cf. *japonica mai*).

izakaya [*izakaya*] (居酒屋 / いざかや) - Any variety of drinking establishments that also has a food menu and a cozy environment. Could be translated as a Japanese gastropub.

Izu Shotō (伊豆 諸島 / いず しょとう) - A group of islands stretching south from Tokyo which have become known for their potato and barley shochu. The islands are administratively a part of Tokyo, and they currently host 10 active distilleries. The potato shochu, which is made with barley *kōji*, has been dubbed "Island Saké" (*shima zake*) by the archipelago's residents.

J

japonica mai (ジャポニカ 米 / じゃぽにか まい) - Strains of rice that are cultivated in relatively temperate climates, including large parts of Japan (cf. *indica mai*).

jōchū - Pronunciation of the word shochu when it is part of some noun phrases. For example, 麦焼酎 / *mugi* shochu is generally pronounced *mugi jochu* in conversation.

jōatsu (常圧 / じょうあつ) – Atmospheric pressure. In the shochu industry, this word refers to atmospheric pressure distillation (*jōatsu jōryū*).

jōryū (蒸留 / じょうりゅう) – Distillation.

joy white (ジョイ ホワイト / じょい ほわいと) - A type of sweet potato (*satsuma im*o) that is often used in shochu production. It has a high starch content and often lends a lemony fruitiness to the aroma of the finished shochu.

jōzō arukōru (醸造 アルコール / じょうぞう あるこーる) - Brewer's alcohol. Ethanol that is around 96% ABV and used in some grades of nihonshu. When diluted to 35% ABV it's called *kōrui* shochu.

K

kana (仮名 or 仮字 / かな) - Collective name for *katakana* and *hiragana*. Refers to Japanese syllabary but excludes *kanji*.

kanji [*kanji*] (漢字 / かんじ) - Logograms/logographs that originated in China and are used in written Japanese to represent many morphemes and full words. Often called Chinese characters, they are used in tandem with *kana* and numbers to construct full sentences. Elementary school students in Japan spend six years learning the roughly 1,000 characters that are deemed necessary to read most newspaper articles.

kansho (甘藷 / かんしょ) - Sweet potato. The two *kanji* used to write this word are now often pronounced *satsuma imo*.

kashidaru chozō (樫樽 貯蔵 / かしだる ちょぞう) - Oak cask aged.

kasutori shochu [*kasutori shōchū* or *kasutori jōchū*] (粕取り 焼酎 / かすとり しょうちゅう) - A type of shochu made by distilling the rice lees from nihonshu fermentation. The result is a shochu with distinct *ginjō* aromas.

katakana (片仮名 / かたかな) - A sharp, angular syllabary used mostly to write words borrowed from other languages (cf. *hiragana*).

ki kōji (黄麹 / き こうじ) - A shortened version of *ki kōji kin*. Indicates that yellow *kōji* mold spores were spread on the starch source to make the *kōji*.

kōbo (酵母 / こうぼ) - Yeast.

koganesengan (黄金千貫 or コガネセンガン / こがねせんが
ん) - The most popular varietal of sweet potato used to make
imo shochu. It packs a high starch content and tends to impart
a sweet earthiness in the resulting shochu.

kōji (麹 / こうじ) - A starch source (rice, barley, etc.) that has
kōji kin living within it. *Kōji* is most commonly made with
rice, and when done by hand (*te'dzukuri*) it is a labor intensive
process that takes nearly two full days (cf. *kōji kin*).

kōji buta (麹 蓋 / こうじ ぶた) - The lids or trays that were
traditionally used during the *kōji* preparation process. The
small trays have been abandoned by larger distilleries, but if
this labor intensive method is used today, then the distillery is
often permitted to print *te'dzukuri* on the label (cf. *te'dzukuri*).

kōji kin (麹菌 / こうじ きん) - Mold spores.

kōji muro (麹 室 / こうじ むろ) - The temperature and humidity-
controlled room in the distillery where *kōji* is prepared.

kokutō (黒糖 / こくとう) - Brown sugar.

kokutō shochu [*kokutō shōchū* or *kokutō jōchū*] (黒糖焼酎 / こ
くとう しょうちゅう) - Brown sugar shochu (cf. Amami *Kokutō*
Shochu).

kome (米 / こめ) - Rice.

kome shochu [*kome shōchū* or *kome jōchū*] (米焼酎 / こめ しょ
うちゅう) - Rice shochu.

konwa shochu (混和焼酎 / こんわ しょうちゅう) - Shochu that
involves a mix of *kōrui* and *otsurui* distillates.

kōrui shochu (甲類焼酎 / こうるい しょうちゅう) - Multiple-distilled shochu that carries a neutral aroma and flavor profile. Often used for cocktail mixing. This type of shochu must not have an ABV exceeding 35% (cf. *otsurui* shochu; *konwa* shochu).

koshu (古酒 / こしゅ) - Shochu that has been aged for at least three years (cf. *chōki chozō* above and *kūsu* below).

kuchikami saké (口噛み 酒 / くちかみ さけ) - Alcohol made by chewing the starch source so that enzymes from human saliva enable saccharification. Effectively replaces the need for creating *kōji*.

Kuma Shochu [*kuma shōchū* or *kuma jōchū*] (球磨 焼酎 / くま しょうちゅう) - WTO-protected appellation of rice shochu made in the Hitoyoshi Basin, Kumamoto Prefecture.

kuri shochu [*kuri shōchū* or *kuri jōchū*] (栗焼酎 / くり しょうちゅう) - Chestnut shochu.

kuro (黒 / くろ) - Black.

kuro joka (黒 ジョカ / くろ じょか) - A small kettle which is used to heat and/or hold shochu.

kuro kōji (黒 麹 / くろ こうじ) - A shortened version of *kuro kōji kin*. Indicates that black *kōji* mold spores were spread on the starch source to make the *kōji*.

kūsu (古酒 / くーす) - Awamori aged for at least three years (cf. *koshu*).

Kyushu [*Kyūshū*] (九州 / きゅうしゅう) - The third largest island of the Japanese archipelago, and most southern of the four main islands. It is the traditional home of shochu as we know it today. It is comprised of seven prefectures: Kagoshima, Miyazaki, Nagasaki, Kumamoto, Oita, Fukuoka, and Saga. The vast majority of honkaku shochu is made in this part of Japan.

M

maewari (前割り / まえわり) - Shochu that has been cut with water a day or more before its intended consumption. This is a serving style popularized by the residents of Kagoshima Prefecture who found that allowing the water and shochu extra time to mingle will result in a softer, rounder drink the next day.

mai (米 / まい) - Rice (cf. *kome*).

makizushi (巻き鮨 / まきずし) - Sushi roll made with *mitsuba*, mushrooms, dried gourd strips, "freeze-dried" tofu, omelet, and sushi rice. Cut into thick wheels and sometimes dipped in soy sauce (cf. *norimaki*).

makgeolli (막걸리) - Korean unfiltered rice and/or wheat alcohol. It has recently become popular in Japan, and you can sometimes find it on menus as *makkori* (マッコリ / まっこり).

mizuwari (水割り / みずわり) - Shochu that has been mixed with water before serving.

moromi (醪 / もろみ) - The fermenting mash. Usually divided into two stages in shochu production. Awamori production involves a single stage of *moromi* fermentation.

mugi (麦 / むぎ) - Barley.

mugi shochu [*mugi shōchū* or *mugi jōchū*] (麦焼酎 / むぎ しょうちゅう) - Barley shochu.

N

nen (年 / ねん) - Year(s).

nihonshu [*nihonshu*] (日本酒 / にほんしゆ) - Known as saké outside of Japan, it's an alcoholic drink made from polished rice which is usually bottled at around 15% ABV.

niji shikomi (二次 仕込み / にじ しこみ) - Second *moromi* fermentation. The *moromi* from the first stage of fermentation is supplemented with the main starch ingredient (potato, barley, etc.) of the finished shochu.

nipponbare (日本晴 / にっぽんばれ) - Also pronounced *nihonbare*, this rice varietal is sometimes used in shochu production.

norimaki (海苔巻き / のりまき) - The general name for a sushi roll, no matter how simple or packed with ingredients. At the very least, sushi rolls contain vinegared rice and one other ingredient rolled in dried seaweed (cf. *makizushi*).

nurukan (ぬる燗 / ぬるかん) - Shochu that has been cut with hot water and served at around 40 degrees Celsius.

O

oolong hai (烏龍 ハイ / うーろん はい) - A popular izakaya cocktail featuring a mixture of oolong tea and shochu.

otsurui shochu (乙類焼酎 / おつるい　しょうちゅう) - A somewhat dated title for single-distilled shochu, it has now mostly been replaced by the term honkaku shochu although the two descriptions are generally still understood as being one and the same (cf. *kōrui* shochu; *konwa* shochu).

oyuwari (お湯割 / おゆわり) - Shochu that has been cut with hot water and served at a temperature that is usually between 50 and 60 degrees Celsius.

P

patent still - Also known as a column still. A type of still that enables continuous distillation or *renzoku jōryū* (連続 蒸留 / れんぞく　じょうりゅう). The result is often a nearly pure ethanol alcohol (around 96% ABV) that has shed the flavors and aromas of the ingredients that were used during fermentation (cf. pot still).

pot still - Also called an alembic. A type of still that collects distillate after a single distillation run or *tanshiki jōryū* (単式 蒸留 / たんしき　じょうりゅう). The result is a relatively low ABV alcohol that retains more of the character of the ingredients that were used during fermentation (cf. patent still)

R

roka (濾過 / ろか) - Filtration.

roku yon (6:4 / ろく　よん) - The standard ratio used for mixing shochu with cool (*mizuwari*) and hot water (*oyuwari*). The first number in the ratio is the shochu, and the second number is the water.

Ryūkyū (琉球 / りゅうきゅう) - Former name of the Okinawan archipelago.

Ryukyu Awamori [*Ryūkyū Awamori*] (琉球 泡盛 / りゅうきゅう あわもり) - Official WTO-protected designation reserved for awamori made in Okinawa.

S

saké (酒 / さけ) - This word means *alcohol* in Japanese, but it is used outside of Japan to refer exclusively to nihonshu. Using this word when visiting Japan can cause confusion because shochu, beer, wine, and whiskey are saké, too. The accent is my own addition to help remind people outside Japan of the correct pronunciation.

Satsuma (薩摩 / さつま) - Former name of southern Kyushu, or what is now Kagoshima Prefecture.

satsuma imo (薩摩芋 or さつま芋 / さつまいも) - Sweet potato.

Satsuma Shochu [*Satsuma Shōchū* or *Satsuma Jōchū*] (薩摩 焼酎 / さつま しょうちゅう) - The WTO-protected designation reserved for *imo* shochu made with local ingredients in Kagoshima Prefecture.

seibaku (精麦 / せいばく) - Barley/wheat polishing.

seigiku (製麹 / せいぎく) - *Kōji* preparation. Also pronounced *seikiku*.

seimaibuai (精米歩合 / せいまいぶあい) - Rice polishing ratio.

seishu (清酒 / せいしゆ) - Alternative and official name for nihonshu. Often printed on bottle labels and menus.

shabu shabu (しゃぶ しゃぶ) - Hotpot dish involving thin strips of beef and vegetables dipped in boiling water or stock.

Thinly sliced pork is also used, and the dish is typically prepared on a burner either in or on the middle of the dining table (cf. *sukiyaki*).

shinshu (新酒 / しんしゅ) - Literally 'new alcohol.' The most recent vintage of a particular alcohol.

shintō (神道 / しんとう) - A Japanese religion whose name can be translated as the "way of the spirits." For the average person living in Japan, the faith involves praying at shrines and asking spirits for assistance with the various obstacles presented in life such as exams and financial woes. There is no god-like figure, and adherents are free to practice other religions simultaneously.

shiro kōji (白麹 / しろ こうじ) - A shortened version of *shiro kōji kin*. Indicates that white *kōji* mold spores were spread on the starch source to make the *kōji*.

shiro yutaka (シロ ユタカ) - A type of sweet potato (*satsuma imo*) that is known for a comparable starch content to the more popular *koganesengan* and a refreshing sweetness.

shiso (紫蘇 / しそ) - Perilla or beefsteak plant. It is a relative of mint, and the green leaves carry understated basil notes. The green leaves are used in tempura, sashimi, and sushi. Red *shiso* leaves, on the other hand, are often used to add color to pickled vegetables and *umeboshi*.

shochu [*shōchū*] (焼酎 / しょうちゅう) - An alcoholic beverage distilled from a mash (*moromi*) made with *kōji*, water, yeast, and additional starch source(s). Written *shōchū* in Revised Hepburn transliteration system. As of May 1st, 2006, shochu is divided and taxed according to the type of still that is used to distill it (cf. patent still; pot still).

shodō (書道 / しょどう) - Calligraphy.

shuzō (酒造 / しゅぞう) - Distillery.

soba (蕎麦 / そば) - Buckwheat. Most often used to refer to buckwheat noodles in Japan.

soba shochu [*soba shōchū* or *soba jōchū*] (蕎麦焼酎 or そば焼酎 / そば しょうちゅう) - Buckwheat shochu.

soju (소주) - A distilled Korean alcoholic beverage that is not dissimilar from multiple-distilled *kōrui* shochu. Due to labeling anomalies in the United States, soju and honkaku shochu are sometimes mistakenly assumed to be the same thing.

sorakyū (そらきゅう) - Small cone-shaped drinking pottery that will spill if you try to put them down. Some styles require extra concentration because they have a small hole in the bottom that the user must plug with their finger until they've finished their drink.

suedare (すえだれ) - The final part of the distillation run. It is usually around 10% ABV, and it is responsible for adding depth to the distillate (cf. *hanatare*).

sukiyaki (鋤焼き / すきやき) - Thinly sliced beef dipped in boiling water, often with soy sauce and *mirin* added to it. Vegetables such as onions and mushrooms, as well as tofu, are often added to the broth. The boiled slices of beef are then dunked in raw egg before eating (cf. *shabu shabu*).

T

tanku (タンク / たんく) - This is the Japanese pronunciation of the word *tank*.

te'dzukuri (手造り / てづくり) - Handmade. *Te'dzukuri* can only be printed on the label if the *kōji* was made using the traditional style in a mostly modern technology-free *kōji muro*. In other words, the temperature and humidity can only be controlled by opening the window in the ceiling (not by electric air conditioning equipment), and *kōji buta* must be used to control the temperature and progress of the *kōji* preparation.

T(h)ai mai (タイ米 / たい まい) - Basically another name for *indica mai*, this type of rice is mostly used to make awamori. However, recently it has become more common to see *Thai mai* used in *kōji* preparation for shochu as well.

toki masari (とき まさり) - A sweet potato (*satsuma imo*) varietal born in 2007 that brings a distinguished sweetness and depth to the finished product. It also boasts a higher alcohol output in the resulting *genshu* than *koganesengan*.

tōji (杜氏 / とうじ) - Master brewer or distiller.

U

umami [*umami*] (旨味 / うまみ) - Roughly translated as 'tastiness' or 'savoriness,' it is one of the five major tastes registered by the tongue. The taste is primarily correlated with monosodium glutamate (MSG) and the sodiums guanylate and inosinate. Food and drink that can draw out this depth of flavor are highly regarded.

ume (梅 / うめ) - Japanese apricot. It is either pickled with salt to make *umeboshi*, or it's used to make umeshu liqueur.

umeshu (梅酒 / うめしゅ) - A liqueur that is made by macerating rock sugar and *ume* in a large jar of *kōrui* shochu. It is a very common homemade liqueur in Japan, and an umeshu recipe can be found at the end of chapter nine of this book.

W
wari (割 / わり) - Cut or mixed with some other liquid.

warimizu (割水 / わりみず) - Sometimes also called *kasui* (加水 / かすい), this is the water that is used to dilute shochu down to its target ABV.

Y
yon gō bin (四 合 瓶 / よん ごう びん) - Standard 720 ml bottle. It is four (*yon*) times the size of the decanter (one *gō* = 180 ml) used to serve shochu and nihonshu in izakaya.

Z
zenkōji shikomi (全麹 仕込み / ぜんこうじ しこみ) - All of the prepared *kōji*, water, and yeast are added to the fermentation tank at the same time. There is only one fermentation stage. *Zenkōji shikomi* is employed in awamori production (cf. awamori).

Further Reading

Sources in English

Although there aren't yet any other books written in English that are specifically about shochu, if you're an *alcademic* like me, then you need to take a few of these for a spin. I have included a couple of nihonshu-specific books just because I have a large amount of respect for the two gentlemen that wrote them, and the drink, like shochu, is inseparable from Japan's gastronomic traditions.

Bunting, Chris. *Drinking Japan.* Tuttle, 2011.

Dornenburg, Andrew, and Karen Page. *What to Drink with What you Eat.* Bulfinch Press, 2006.

Gauntner, John. *The Saké Handbook.* Tuttle, 2002.

Harper, Philip. *The Insider's Guide to Saké.* Kodansha International, 1998.

Hosking, Richard. *A Dictionary of Japanese Food.* Tuttle, 1995.

Sakamoto, Yukari. *Food Sake Tokyo.* Little Bookroom, 2010.

Allow me to include one online resource here as well. Quoted in chapter seven, Stephen Lyman's website (http://kampai.us/) is well worth consulting when buying shochu that has found its way to a retailer outside of Japan. He is just as passionate about shochu as I am, so bookmark his website because it will continue to grow.

Sources in Japanese

This list is naturally longer due to the fact that the bulk of what is written about shochu and awamori has occurred in Japanese. Several of these books were invaluable to my ability to cross-check the information that I have unearthed during my research and travels.

Hashiguchi, Takashi. *Honkaku Shochu.* (*Japanese Shochu Catalog & Bible.*) Shinsei, 2004.

Honkaku Shochu Teisutingu BOOK. (*Honkaku Shochu Tasting Book.*) X Knowledge, 2005.

Ikkojin Henshūbu (Ikkojin Editorial Department.) *Umai! Honkaku Shochu Nomikurabe.* (*Delicious! Honkaku Shochu Tasting.*) Best Sellers, 2004.

Ina, Yasuyuki. *Shochu 1,891 Shu.* (*Shochu Data Book.*) Seibundō Shinkōsha, 2009.

Nagata, Taku. *Shochu Techō.* (*Shochu Encyclopedia for Gourmet.*) Tokyo Shoseki, 2010.

Nihon Shurui Kenkyūkai. *Shochu Nyūmon.* (*The First Book of Tasting Shochu.*) Gentosha, 2009.

Roswell, Hosoki. *Shochu 100 Era.* (*100 Shochu Selections.*) Nihon Bungeisha, 2012.

Satō, Yorihisa. *Nihonshu to Shochu no Baiburu.* (*The Nihonshu and Shochu Bible.*)

Shochu / Awamori Handobukku. (*Shochu / Awamori Handbook.*) Ikeda Shoten, 2008.

Shochu no Motoi. (*Shochu Fundamentals.*) Saké Service Institute (SSI), 2010.

Sumi, Kenji. *Shochu no Kimoto.* (*The Basics of Sh*ochu.) Ei Publishing Company, Ltd., 2010.

Tateyama, Masao. *Honkaku Shochu / Awamori Handobukku.* (*Honkaku Shochu / Awamori Handbook.*) Nikkei BP Kikaku, 2005.

Author Biography

Christopher Pellegrini, known by his colleagues at Japan Eats (http://japaneats.tv/) as the "Shochu Whisperer," is a leading expert on all things shochu and awamori (http://shochu.pro/). Based in Tokyo, Japan, he gives shochu lectures and provides menu consulting for izakaya and Japanese restaurants worldwide. He is an officially licensed and registered Shochu Sommelier with the SSI (Sake Service Institute) and FBO (Food & Beverage Specialists Organization).

Pellegrini is also the English translator for the survival-Japanese textbook, "Konnichiwa, Nihongo!" and the regular host of "Ishokudōgen," a show that seeks to introduce Japanese culinary culture abroad. He holds an MA in language education from UCL's Institute of Education and loves his family and friends in Vermont dearly.

Contact the author:

Follow Christopher Pellegrini on Twitter (@ChrisPellegrini) for continuing commentary on shochu and awamori.